GUITAR WORLD PRESENTS

METALLICA

GUITAR WORLD PRESENTS

METALLICA

FROM THE PAGES OF

GUITAR WORLD

MAGAZINE

Backbeat
Books

AN IMPRINT OF HAL LEONARD CORPORATION

NEW YORK

Articles by Steffan Chirazi, Dan Epstein, Jeff Gilbert, Jeff Spurrier, Jaan Uhelszki and
Mick Wall used by permission.

Published in 2010 by Backbeat Books
An Imprint of Hal Leonard Corporation
7777 West Bluemound Road
Milwaukee, WI 53213

Trade Book Division Editorial Offices
19 West 21st Street, New York, NY 10010

Printed in the United States of America

Executive Producer: Brad Tolinski
Editors: Jeff Kitts, Brad Tolinski, Chris Scapelliti
Art Director: Alexis Cook
Photo Editors: Jimmy Hubbard, Samantha Xu
Cover Photograph: Ross Halfin

Library of Congress Cataloging-in-Publication data is available upon request.

ISBN 978-0-87930-970-1

www.backbeatbooks.com

CONTENTS

GUITAR WORLD PRESENTS

METALLICA

[1]

"A part of Metallica
was lost forever
when Cliff died."
—*KIRK HAMMETT*

ENCYCLOPEDIA METALLICA

An A-to-Z overview of the most magnificent
metal act of all time.

BY ALAN DI PERNA

ALL THROUGHOUT R♦CK HISTORY there have been bands that started out as concepts before they ever became bands. Some guy has an idea and then goes out and assembles a bunch of musicians to embody that idea. The Monkees, the Spice Girls and the Sex Pistols are three notable instances. It's a common scenario, although one that rarely occurs in metal. The quintessential metal band's bio is usually a tale of four or five mooks who start out in a garage somewhere, make derivative noise for a while and then slowly discover an identity.

Metallica are metal's notable exception to this paradigm. The whole thing began with drummer Lars Ulrich's unquenchable urge to have a band. He secured a record deal for the entity that would

Editor's note: This article contains passages that appear elsewhere in this book.

become Metallica long before the now-celebrated lineup—featuring guitar legends Kirk Hammett and James Hetfield—was in place, and long before he was even very good behind a drum kit. The irrepressible drummer pretty much willed Metallica into being. He's got that kind of energy.

But most concept bands are short lived. They tend to last only as long as the pop culture moment that gave rise to the concept that gave rise to them. And here's where Metallica pull away from the pack.

Now in their third decade of existence, Metallica have become one of the greatest metal acts of all time, right up there in the pantheon with Led Zeppelin, Van Halen, Ozzy and all the others. One key to their longevity is the fact that they've fearlessly altered their style as they've evolved, which is also a relative rarity in the world of metal.

Metallica started out as champions of the early Eighties thrash metal scene, a genre that they played a large role in inventing. But they soon moved on from there, drawing cries of "sellout" from disaffected punters while attracting larger and larger audiences. As of this writing, they've sold more than 90 million records worldwide. Their very name has become synonymous with the metal genre itself.

"The cool thing about Metallica is that there's always a new generation of angry young men who latch onto *Kill 'Em All* and know what I'm talking about," Hetfield says. "We've never been about creating some fantasy world with our records; we're just documenting where we're at at the time. There's always going to be youth on the planet. And every time I look out in the crowd and see some kids battling it out in the middle of the mosh pit, I'm like, Yeah, I was there, man."

The Metallica story is a classic metal band saga, replete with revolving door personnel changes, tragic death, trashed recording studios, stints in rehab, career peaks and valleys and, of course, loads of the most thunderous, aggressive and heaviest music the world has ever known.

GARAGE DAYS

THE WHOLE THING BEGAN, as mentioned, with Lars Ulrich, the Danish-born son of tennis pro Torben Ulrich. Lars' original life ambition was to follow in his father's footsteps. The family even moved from Denmark to Los Angeles so that Lars could pursue a career in tennis. But when the New Wave of British Heavy Metal (NWOBHM) scene exploded out of the U.K. in the late Seventies, spearheaded by bands like Iron Maiden, Judas Priest, Saxon and Motörhead, the 16-year-old found his true calling. He wanted to be part of this new metal scene any way he could. He traveled to England to follow NWOBHM frontrunners Diamond Head from gig to gig, befriending the band's lead guitarist Brian Tatler. He also helped Geoff Barton, editor of U.K. metal mag *Kerrang!*, put together a compilation of NWOBHM bands.

But Ulrich wasn't content to cheer metal on from the sidelines. Back home in L.A. in 1981, he placed an advertisement in *The Recycler*, a local classified ads paper, canvassing for other musicians to jam with and listing the Tygers of Pan Tang, Diamond Head and Iron Maiden as his influences. One of those who replied to his ad was James Hetfield, a young guitarist who'd fallen in love with rock and metal, despite being raised in a strict Christian Scientist family. Hetfield had already had some experience playing with local bands bearing marginally risible names like Obsession, Phantom Lord and Leather Charm. Hetfield's initial jam with Ulrich, which also included Leather Charm guitarist Hugh Tanner, was something less than spectacular.

"Lars had a pretty crappy drum kit, with one cymbal that kept falling over," Hetfield recalls. "We'd have to stop playing and he'd pick the fucking thing up. He really was not a good drummer."

But Ulrich has never been one to give up easily. He'd befriended another metal enthusiast, Brian Slagel, who edited an early fanzine called *The New Heavy Metal Review*. Slagel was planning to release a compilation album to be titled *The New Heavy Metal Review Presents Metal Massacre*, and Lars persuaded Slagel to let him have a track on the album, tactfully omitting to mention that he didn't actually have a band, nor even any written material to record.

Armed with Slagel's promise, Ulrich went back to Hetfield, who was seduced by the idea of having a track on an actual, real record album. And so Ulrich and Hetfield, together with a guitarist named Lloyd Grant and a bassist named Ron McGovney, knocked out the first-ever Metallica recording, "Hit the Lights," which was duly released on the *Metal Massacre* compilation in 1981.

The story of how the band got the name Metallica offers another example of Ulrich's ability not to let scruples stand in the way of his hard-driven ambition. One of Lars' friends at the time was a radio DJ named Ron Quintana, who was planning to start his own fanzine. He was vacillating between two possible names that he had devised for the publication. One was *Metal Mania* and the other was *Metallica*. Ulrich promptly persuaded him that *Metal Mania* was the way to go, leaving Lars free to pinch Metallica for his own fledgling band. Creative borrowing is, after all, the engine that drives rock history. In all likelihood, Quintana himself had lifted the name from the *Encyclopedia Metallica*, a metal reference book that had just been published at the time (and the name of which was adapted from the venerable research resource the *Encyclopedia Britannica*).

The early Metallica lineup was unstable to say the least. Lloyd Grant didn't even last long enough play the band's first gig. His place was taken by Dave Mustaine, a talented and outspoken newcomer at the time. By this point Ron McGovney had already surrendered the bass slot to Cliff Burton from the band Trauma, whom the Metallica guys had seen perform at the Whisky in L.A.

James Hetfield fondly remembers Burton as "a wild, hippie-ish, acid-taking, bell-bottom-wearing guy. He meant business and you couldn't fuck around with him. I wanted to get the respect that he had." Burton would prove to be a key member of Metallica and had a large impact on the band's early style and direction. One of his first moves was to induce the band to relocate to his home city of San Francisco, saying he wouldn't join Metallica unless they made the move.

Dave Mustaine's tenure in Metallica lasted until 1983, when he was kicked out of the band for drunken unreliability shortly after insulting guitar virtuoso Adrian Vandenberg at a soundcheck at the L'amour club in Brooklyn. He would of course go on to fame at the helm of Megadeth. Taking Mustaine's place on lead guitar was Kirk Hammett, a veteran of the band Exodus and a former guitar student of Joe Satriani. Ulrich, Hetfield and Burton persuaded Hammett to make his blinding technique a part of Metallica.

"I was familiar with Metallica's music before I joined the band," Hammett recalls. "Exodus played with Metallica pretty often in San Francisco. The first time I spoke to Lars was after they had just finished a set and I said, 'Thanks for letting us play. I really like you guys.' He said, 'Yeah, yeah, cool, cool.' But as I was talking to him, he started taking his stage clothes off, and before I knew it, he was completely naked in front of me. I was just shocked. I said to myself. 'Oh he's European. Europeans do stuff like this.' "

Ulrich, in turn, responded to the naked emotion in Hammett's playing. "I remember the first time I heard Kirk," the drummer recollects. "He had a feel that very few young players have—very rooted in European metal. It was really nice to hear an American guy who didn't play like Eddie Van Halen."

A KILLER DEBUT

VARIOUS EARLY METALLICA lineups had recorded several influential demos, including the *Power Metal* and *No Life Till Leather* recordings. This landed Metallica a deal on Megaforce Records. And in the spring of 1983 Metallica descended on Music America Studios in Rochester, New York, to record their debut album, *Kill 'Em All*, with producer Paul Curico.

"I remember the first time I heard Kirk. It was really nice to hear an American guy who didn't play like Eddie Van Halen."
—*ULRICH*

"We totally trashed the place," Hammett says with a laugh. "I felt bad. But we were four young guys, you know? There was carpet in every single room, and we drank pretty much 24 hours a day back then. So you can imagine how that turned out. Moist places shouldn't have rugs."

And then there was trouble with the kind of spirits that don't come out of a bottle. "The place was fucking haunted!" Ulrich says. "The actual studio was in the basement of this huge old colonial type of clubhouse. On the second floor there was a huge ballroom; perfect for getting a good drum sound. The problem was my cymbals would start spinning around for no reason. Shit like that would happen. It was scary."

There was also the spectre of Dave Mustaine to contend with. He'd only departed the band about three months before the *Kill 'Em All* sessions began and had written some of the material that Metallica were working up in the studio. "Dave brought the song 'The Four Horsemen' over from one of his other bands," Hetfield says. "Back then it was called 'The Mechanix.' After he left Metallica, we kind of fixed the song up. The lyrics he used were pretty silly."

Hammett attributes much of the tough-as-nails guitar sound on *Kill 'Em All* to "James' magical, mythical Marshall. All the guitar stuff was recorded through that. He'd had it modified by some guy in L.A. who used to work on Eddie Van Halen's gear. I used it too because we didn't have much equipment back then. I played my black Flying V and James used his white Flying V. Those were the only guitars we had. I also used a wah pedal and Boss Super Distortion."

"It was Cliff who named the album," Hetfield adds. "Originally we were supposed to call it *Metal Up Your Ass*. We got a phone call from our manager telling us half the record outlets wouldn't carry the album if we called it that. Cliff said, 'You know what? Fuck those fuckers, man. We should just kill 'em all.' "

The album, released on July 25, 1983, became one of the first major statements of a burgeoning new genre called "thrash metal." An amalgam of NWOBHM and hardcore punk, thrash metal was very much an underground phenomenon at the time. Mainstream rock attention in the early Eighties was divided between new wave/post-punk/synth-pop acts like the Police, U2, the Cure, Talking Heads and Depeche Mode on the one hand and the more accessible metal sounds of acts like Van Halen and Ozzy Osbourne on the other. Thrash metal was hardly on the radar, but the genre's lightning-fast tempos hit a responsive note with a growing subculture of hyperactive, testosterone-crazed adolescent males.

"Part of the reason why we would play so fast is because we were just nervous," Hammett says. "As a young musician, when I was nervous I had a tendency to speed things up. Joining Metallica, I thought, This is great, because it can never be too fast."

"Lars was always nervous onstage," Hetfield adds, "so he'd just play faster and faster. Nobody wanted to wimp out and tell him. We figured, 'Hell, we'll just play faster too.' And that's what we did on the record as well."

MAJOR-LABEL ASCENDANCY

SOLID SALES OF *KILL 'EM ALL* did not go unnoticed by Elektra Records. The label signed Metallica, which made them the first thrash metal act to be picked up by a major label. By this point the band had already finished recording its second album, *Ride the Lightning*, at Sweet Silence Studios in Copenhagen, Denmark. At the production helm was Flemming Rasmussen, who would become an important member of the team for the next few Metallica albums. When *Ride the Lightning* hit the streets in fall of 1984, it marked a significant creative step forward for the band.

"Cliff Burton was responsible for a lot of the things that happened between *Kill 'Em All* and *Ride the Lightning*," says Ulrich. "Cliff really exposed James and me to a whole new musical horizon of harmonies and melodies. [*Our*] whole way of writing songs together was very much shaped around Cliff's musical input."

> "Lars was always nervous onstage, so he'd just play faster and faster."
> —HETFIELD

"'Creeping Death' was our first big chanting, gang-vocal song," Hetfield adds. "There was almost some production value to it!"

The band's guitar sound was evolving too, according to Kirk Hammett. "I tracked the whole album with Marshall amps and my Gibson Flying V," he says. "And by then James had his Gibson Explorer."

Ride the Lightning is also memorable for containing what is often hailed as the world's first thrash metal ballad, "Fade to Black." "It's a suicide song," says Hetfield, "and we got a lot of flack for that, [*as if*] kids were killing themselves because of the song. But we also got hundreds and hundreds of letters from kids telling us how they related to the song and that it made them feel better. It was also pretty much our first ballad, so it was challenging and we knew it would freak people out. Bands like Exodus and Slayer don't do ballads, but they've stuck themselves in that position, which is something we've never wanted to do. Limiting yourself to please your audience is bullshit."

By the mid-Eighties, thanks to proper tour support, promotion and other key financial backing from Elektra, Metallica were starting to have a significant impact on the mainstream. They worked their way up the ladder on the metal festival circuit, playing to more than 70,000 happy punters at the Monsters of Rock fest in Donnington, England, in 1985. In September, they once again entered Denmark's Sweet Silence Studios with producer Flemming Rasmussen and emerged with one of their all-time classic albums: *Master of Puppets*. Bruising anthems like "Battery," "Damage, Inc." and "Disposable Heroes" have become essential repertoire for aspiring metal guitarists, not to mention the album's title track. The signature descending riff in "Master of Puppets" grew out of dressing room jams that took place on the *Ride the Lightning* tour.

"James would always play that riff, but on the D string," Hammett recalls. "And I'd play it simultaneously on the G string as a parallel-fourths harmony line. It sounded really dorky and funny. Then, one day at rehearsal, James said, 'Let me show you this really heavy song intro,' and proceeded to play that exact riff on the low E string.' I said, 'Ah, so you finally found a use for that dorky little thing!' It's anything but dorky now.

"I used a Mesa/Boogie Mark II-C head and my Jackson Randy Rhoads V on 'Master of Puppets,' " Hammett goes on to explain. "When you listen to the solo, there's this weird sound right after the mellow part, where it sounds like I'm hitting a super high note, like I'm fretting the string against the pickup. What happened was, I accidentally pulled the string off the fretboard and it fretted out on the side of the neck! I heard it back and was, like, 'That's brilliant! We've gotta keep that!' Of course I've never been able to reproduce it since."

THE DARKEST NIGHT

RELEASED ON MARCH 3, 1986, *Master of Puppets* sold half a million copies in a matter of months, giving Metallica their first Gold record and peaking at Number 29 on the *Billboard* album chart. A high profile tour with Ozzy Osbourne further increased the band's visibility. Things had never looked better for Metallica. But then, in the fall of 1986, the band suffered a grievous loss while on the European leg of their Damage, Inc. tour. On September 27, while traveling to a show in Copenhagen, Denmark, the band's tour bus went into a skid and veered off the road near Dorap, Sweden. The vehicle flipped over several times. Cliff Burton was asleep in his bunk at the time and was thrown through one of the bus windows. The vehicle then landed on top of his body, killing him instantly.

James Hetfield will forever be haunted by what he saw and experienced that night. "I saw the bus lying right on him," he says. "I saw his legs sticking out. I went to pieces. The driver tried to take

Cliff's blanket and give it to someone else. I just screamed, 'Fuck that!' I wanted to kill the guy. I don't know if he was drunk or if the bus had skidded on ice. All I knew was Cliff was dead."

Burton was only 24 years old at the time of his passing, but he'd already made an indelible mark on metal history. "A part of Metallica was lost forever when Cliff died," Hammett says.

For a few grief-stricken weeks, it seemed like the end of Metallica. Hetfield was particularly against the idea of continuing without Burton. "The only thing I could think was, The band? No way. There ain't no band. The band is not that band right now. It's just three guys."

But in time, they decided to soldier on. After auditioning more than 60 bass players, they decided on Jason Newsted of the band Flotsam and Jetsam. The 23-year-old bassman faced a formidable challenge in attempting to fill the void left by the death of the well-loved Burton.

"When I came into Metallica, I had to do justice to Cliff's work, but I also had to put my own signature on it," Newsted says. "No one could be Cliff Burton; Cliff Burton was the Jimi Hendrix of bass. I had to practice, practice, practice to get anywhere close to where he was."

The band started back slowly with an EP of metal covers titled *The $5.98 E.P.: Garage Days Re-Revisited*. It was hardly a major work, but Elektra were happy to have some new Metallica product to put on the market. The EP marks the first recording on which Kirk Hammett used ESP guitars with EMG pickups. It would prove to be a long lasting association, with EMG instruments becoming a cornerstone of Hammett and Hetfield's tone in the years that followed.

ROUGH JUSTICE

BY JANUARY 1988 METALLICA were ready to get back to work for real. Once again they got together with producer Flemming Rasmussen.

Only this time recording took place in North Hollywood, at One on One Studios. These sessions would yield the fourth Metallica album and another essential item in the band's catalog, ...And Justice for All. Rarely, if ever, does a metal guitar interview take place without this record being cited. In particular, tracks like "Blackened" and "Harvester of Sorrow" are held in high reverence. Containing nine songs that together clock in at more than an hour, ...And Justice for All is generally hailed as Metallica's most progressive and technically challenging work.

"Things changed after Cliff's death," Hammett explains. Even our sound changed. On Justice we fell prey to that whole virtuosic, late-Eighties thing that was happening. All of a sudden, everyone wanted to be progressive and show off their abilities. Somehow, just playing fast and heavy took a back seat to that."

One band member not particularly well favored on the recording was Jason Newsted. His bass was often buried in the final mix of ...And Justice for All. The bassist found himself in a difficult position. He became an object of resentment for fans who missed Burton. And it seems that he did not receive 100 percent support from his bandmates either. Newsted's tenure in Metallica would prove to be a troubled one, and he would eventually leave the band in 2001.

"There was a lot of anguish after Cliff died, and basically Jason was the punching bag," Hammett admits. "We vented so much on him, and it really wasn't fair."

But all the suffering ultimately led to a success breakthrough that was partly driven by the band's video clip for the single "One." The first Metallica video ever, it became an MTV staple. ...And Justice for All went Platinum within three months of its release on September 6, 1988, and climbed all the way to Number Six on the Billboard album chart. Metallica garnered a Grammy nomination for Best Rock/Heavy

Metal Performance, but infamously lost to Jethro Tull, whose late Sixties and Seventies work certainly contained a proto-metal, riff-driven element but whom almost nobody would think of as a metal band. Metallica capitalized on the irony of the situation by affixing a sticker onto post–Grammy Award copies of ...*And Justice for All* that read "Grammy Award LOSERS."

WHERE BLACK IS THE COLOR AND ONE IS THE NUMBER

TOURING BEHIND THE MASSIVELY popular ...*And Justice for All* lasted into late 1990. It wasn't until October of that year that Metallica were able to get into One on One Studios once again. But this time a new producer was in charge. The place that Flemming Rasmussen had long held was now occupied by Bob Rock, who was best known for producing commercially viable metal acts like Bon Jovi and Mötley Crüe. Rock and Metallica spent nearly a year in the studio and spent a million dollars recording the landmark metal disc that would come to be known as the Black Album, thanks to its extremely dark cover art. (The real title is simply *Metallica*.) It holds roughly the same place of esteem in the metal world that the Beatles' White Album holds for rock and roll fans.

The Black Album is notable for its shorter, more accessible songs, concise riffing and melodic vocals. All these elements became a factor in the album's rampant sales performance. But some diehard metal fans, many of whom had been following Metallica since the days of thrash, felt betrayed. Many reviled Bob Rock as the culprit behind Metallica's lapse into tunefulness, but James Hetfield rejects this notion out of hand.

"People will be saying Bob Rock made Metallica sound like Bon Jovi," he notes. "They don't realize that no one screws with us except us."

"One thing that Bob should be given total credit for," Ulrich says, "is making James comfortable enough to take his guard down and really sing. We've always thought of ourselves as 'Big Bad Metallica,' but Bob taught us a new word that none of us had heard before: 'soulful.'"

While nobody would ever confuse Metallica with James Brown, they did take a more organic approach to the grooves. "What we really wanted was a live feel," Hetfield says. "In the past, Lars and I constructed with rhythm parts without Kirk and Jason. This time, I wanted to try playing as a band unit in the studio. It lightens things up and you get more of a vibe."

This musical strategy allowed Jason Newsted to come into his own on the Black Album. "The bass sound is much weightier," he says. "I tried to create a real rhythm section rather than a one-dimensional sound, and let the guitars do their work. I'm glad the rest of the band could tell me that's what was needed."

By the time the Black Album was recorded, Hammett had evolved a highly specialized, frequency-dependent approach to his guitar tone. "I used a Bradshaw preamp for the lows and mids and a couple of Marshalls for the nice clean highs," he explains. "We EQed it through the board a little bit, and it worked out great. And I used two guitars, a Strat-style ESP with two EMG pickups and an '89 Les Paul Deluxe with two EMGs."

As for Hetfield's tone, "we tried a bunch of amps," he recalls, "but I ended up using the same Mesa/Boogie Mark II Simul Class that I'd used on the previous three albums. My primary guitar was my ESP Explorer with EMGs, but I also used a Telecaster at Gretsch White Falcon with the Bigsby and a Guild 12-string."

The Black Album's lead track, "Enter Sandman," has become a metal classic. Kirk Hammett reveals that he purloined the guitar lick before the breakdown from the song "Magic Man," by Heart. "But I didn't get it [*directly*] from Heart's version," he adds. "I got it from a cut off Ice-T's *Power* album. I was listening to *Power* a lot while we were recording *Metallica*, so I kept on hearing that lick. I thought, I have to snake this! I did change it around a little bit, though."

"Enter Sandman" was the first of six hit singles from the Black Album, which also include "The Unforgiven," "Wherever I May Roam" and the acoustic ballad "Nothing Else Matters." The Black Album became Metallica's first Number One record. It sold 600,000 copies within the first week of its release in August of 1991. Since that time it has gone on to sell more than 22 million and win three Grammys for the band.

Metallica had now fully penetrated and infiltrated the mainstream. The pop-culture moment was right for them. In the early Nineties the Seattle grunge movement had eclipsed hair metal as the hard rock genre of choice, accustoming listeners to a more raw sound. Grunge had also displaced the more arty and pop-oriented aspects of Eighties alternative rock. The entire rock universe became more metal-centric starting in the Nineties. What better rulers for this new metal hegemony than a band name Metallica?

"You think one day some fucker's going to tell you, 'You have a Number One record in America' and the world will ejaculate," Ulrich says. "But I stood there in my hotel room, and there was this fax that said, 'You're Number One.' And it was like, Well, okay. It was just another fucking fax from the office."

LOADED, RE-LOADED AND RUNNING OUT OF AMMUNITION

THE TOURING CYCLE FOR THE Black Album was even more protracted and demanding than it had been for *...And Justice for All*. So it wasn't until 1995 that Metallica got back into the studio with Bob Rock to record a follow-up to the Black Album. When you've hit the top, however, they say the only way to go is down. The band seemed a little unfocussed at the time. There was ambitious talk of making a double album, but what was released in June 1996 was a single disc, *Load*. It met with a mixed reception. Some diehard metal fans found it pretentious. Others were horrified that band wore makeup for the album photo shoot. There was a lurking sense that Metallica were starting to lose the plot. Or maybe they just weren't giving their all anymore.

"We've nearly killed each other and others around us when we've made records before," Ulrich commented at the time. "I think we all felt that we wanted to see if we could come out of this somewhat alive."

The following year saw the release of *Re-Load*, comprised of previously unissued tracks culled from the *Load* sessions. It was hard not to view it as an album of outtakes—B material retrieved from the cutting room floor. But Metallica, and some of their devoted fans, preferred to view it as the second disc in the double album the band had been planning to make ever since the *Load* sessions began.

"We wrote 27 songs for *Load* and were developing it as a double album," says Ulrich. "As far as I'm concerned, you can take any of those songs and interchange them between the two albums."

Then came *S&M* in 1999. A recording of a performance Metallica gave earlier that year in tandem with the San Francisco Symphony Orchestra, it offered up symphonic versions of classic Metallica songs, under the baton of Michael Kamen, who had previously worked with rock artists like Pink Floyd, Aerosmith, Eric Clapton, Queen, David Bowie, Queensrÿche and Def Leppard. While some fans enjoyed hearing Metallica's gnarly arrangements transposed onto orchestral instruments, detractors flashed the "pretentious" card and also dismissed the disc as an attempt to coast on past achievements.

The new century dawned dimly for Metallica. The band's 2000 copyright infringement lawsuit against Napster and aggressive stance against illegal downloading put them in bad odor with the internet generation. And then, in January 2001, Jason Newsted quit the band, squeezing off a devastating parting shot. "What they are doing now is such an obvious cash thing," he said of his former bandmates; "and has nothing to do with the music that we're supposed to be fighting for."

So Bob Rock himself picked up the bass when the band entered the studio with him in April 2001 to begin work on the album that would become *St. Anger*. The process was a difficult one and wound up taking several years. James Hetfield checked into a rehab facility in July 2001 to deal with substance abuse issues. A documentary filmed during the *St. Anger* sessions, and later released under the title *Some Kind of Monster*, chronicled the band's rudderless state.

"It was the fact that there were no real songs," Bob Rock later admitted. "That was because the guy who writes the songs [*Hetfield*] couldn't do it because of what he was going through personally."

Still the band had sufficient career momentum and fanbase loyalty to put *St. Anger* at the top of the U.S. charts when it was released in June 2003. Shortly after the album's release, the band drafted ex Suicidal Tendencies and Ozzy Osbourne bassist Robert Trujillo to fill Metallica's vacant bass slot. He joined just as touring behind *St. Anger* was about to commence.

DEATH AND RESURRECTION

METALLICA MEANT BUSINESS WHEN they converged on Sound City Studios in L.A.'s San Fernando Valley in 2007. There was no denying that their fortunes had slipped somewhat during the late Nineties and early 2000s. They needed to make an album that would put them back on top. "We knew that we needed to go down a different avenue," says Hammett.

Bob Rock was out of the picture. In his place was überproducer and music-biz mastermind Rick Rubin—an ideal choice given Rubin's talent for 11th-hour career resurrection, a feat he'd performed in the past for artists like Johnny Cash and Neil Diamond. But Rubin also knows a thing or two about metal and hard rock, having produced important discs for Slayer, Danzig, the Red Hot Chili Peppers and AC/DC. In fact the Metallica guys had first met Rubin in 1986, just after he'd finished producing Slayer's *Reign in Blood*.

And now Metallica were in the studio with Rubin, looking for a direction home, to paraphrase Bob Dylan. The bearded, guru-like producer advised them, "Imagine that you're not Metallica. You don't have any hits to play, and you have to come up with material to play in a battle of the bands. What do you sound like?"

Thus liberated from the burden of their past, the band came up with *Death Magnetic*, an album that consolidates many of Metallica's timeless strengths while it points a way toward the future. "The new songs are all over the place," Ulrich enthused at the time of the album's release in September 2008. "There's a lot of variation. A lot of fast, slow, melodic...kind of hardcore, nutty super-fast speed stuff. It's a little more like how some of the earlier records were, a little more dynamic within the songs."

The public seems to agree. *Death Magnetic* debuted at Number One at the time of its release and has sold nearly two million copies to date. Twenty-nine years down the road from their inception, Metallica are currently at a new career plateau.

[2]

"Cliff Burton was the
Jimi Hendrix of bass.
I had to practice, practice, practice to get
anywhere close to where he was."
—*JASON NEWSTED*

TALKIN' THRASH

Metallica and a cast of their metal brethren deliver an oral history of the group's first decade: from *Kill 'Em All* to the Black Album.

BY RICHARD BIENSTOCK

IT WAS IN LOS ANGELES almost 30 years ago that Lars Ulrich, a teenage tennis prodigy turned drummer, first jammed with James Hetfield, a guitarist and singer from the nearby SoCal neighborhood of Downey. At the time, a none-too-impressed Hetfield figured that first session to be their last. He was, of course, very wrong. As the backbone of Metallica, Hetfield and Ulrich have gone on to perform countless times for millions of fans around the world and to sell many millions of albums.

All of which would not have been possible without the major players who have passed through the band's ranks over the years, among them guitarist Dave Mustaine, bassist Jason Newsted and, perhaps most crucial, the late, great bassist Cliff Burton. But no single

Editor's note: This article contains passages that appear elsewhere in this book.

musician has been beside Hetfield and Ulrich longer than leadguitarist Kirk Hammett, who joined Metallica prior to the recording of their 1983 debut, *Kill 'Em All*, and whose quick-fingered, melodic soloing is an indispensable element of the band's sound to this day.

Currently rounded out by bassist Robert Trujillo, Metallica released their ninth studio effort, *Death Magnetic*, in September 2008. The album is widely regarded as a return to the band's thrash metal roots, which makes this an ideal moment to tell the story of those trailblazing early days.

In this exclusive oral history, Hetfield, Hammett and Ulrich, along with some friends and former band mates, look back on Metallica's first decade, and recount the recording of their classic first five albums. Through the eyes of those who saw it, heard it, and helped to create the timeless music, *Guitar World* charts Metallica's rise from L.A. thrash upstarts to reigning biggest heavy metal band in the world.

IN THE BEGINNING

In 1980, 16-year-old Lars Ulrich moves with his family from his native Denmark to Los Angeles. Inspired by Deep Purple and New Wave of British Heavy Metal acts like Diamond Head, Saxon and Motörhead, Ulrich puts down his tennis racket, picks up a pair of drumsticks and decides to form a band. Among the first people he meets after moving to L.A. is Brian Slagel, a Southern California teen who would go on to found the independent record label Metal Blade.

BRIAN SLAGEL Lars would always say, "I'm going to start a band one day," and I'd be like, "Sure man, whatever." He had this little drum set in the corner of his bedroom, but it wasn't even set up. I'd always laugh when I saw it because it was just a big mess. But when I started putting together *Metal Massacre* [*the Metal Blade compilation of local, unsigned metal bands*] Lars came to me and said, "If I get a band together, can I be on the album?" Since he was a good friend I said, "Absolutely."

In the summer of 1980, Ulrich places a classified ad in SoCal paper **The Recycler: "Drummer looking for other musicians to jam with, Tygers of Pan Tang, Diamond Head, Iron Maiden."** *Guitarist James Hetfield is among the respondents.*

JAMES HETFIELD The first time Lars and I got together to jam, it just didn't happen. There was no vibe. But he introduced me to a whole new world of heavy music. I had heard of Iron Maiden and Def Leppard but not too many of the other, more obscure English metal bands. I would spend days just going through his record collection, taping over my REO Speedwagon cassettes with bands like Angel Witch and Diamond Head and Motörhead. I was in heaven at his house.

SLAGEL When Lars heard about the *Metal Massacre* compilation I was putting together, the two of them recorded "Hit the Lights" on a little Fostex cassette, and they had their friend, Lloyd Grant, who was a guitar teacher, come in and do the lead.

HETFIELD Lars came to me with the opportunity to be on a record, and that was pretty interesting. At that point in my life I wanted to play music. I didn't want to work.

Ulrich steals the name Metallica from friend and radio DJ Ron Quintana, who had mentioned it as a possible title for a fanzine he was preparing to launch. Ulrich and Hetfield recruit bassist Ron McGovney, who had played with Hetfield previously in the band Leather Charm, and lead guitarist Dave Mustaine to fill out the band's lineup.

DAVE MUSTAINE Before the [*first*] rehearsal, I went to Lars' house, and he played me the tape of "Hit the Lights." I said, "This song sucks. You need more guitar solos." And Lars went, "Oh fuck, *reeeeaaallly?*" I convinced him that I should be in the band and went to rehearsal. I was tuning up when all the other guys went into another room. They weren't talking to me, so I went in and said, "What the fuck? Am I in the band or not?" And they said, "You've got the gig." It was as easy as that.

KERRY KING (Slayer guitarist) I remember seeing Dave play with Metallica at the Woodstock in Anaheim [*California*]. He was ripping these killer solos and riffs, and he was just glaring at the crowd—not even looking at his fingers. I was blown away.

In the spring of 1982 the Hetfield-Ulrich-Mustaine-McGovney line-up records a four-song demo with a new version of "Hit the Lights." The tape comes to be known as the "Power Metal" demo due to business cards McGovney prints up with the phrase at the time.

RON McGOVNEY Lars said, "What did you do! What the hell is 'power metal'? I can't believe you did such a stupid thing!" He was so pissed off at me.

In late 1982, while trying to replace McGovney, Ulrich and Hetfield spot bassist Cliff Burton onstage with his band, Trauma, at the Whisky a Go Go in L.A. The two ask him to join Metallica. Burton agrees, on the condition that the band relocates to his hometown of San Francisco.

SLAGEL Metallica had a lot of problems in L.A. because all the club owners thought they were either too heavy or too punk. They went over so much better in San Francisco than they ever did in their hometown.

GARY HOLT (Exodus guitarist) When they first came to the Bay Area, L.A. was known for nothing more than a lot of shit bands. And then here comes this band, and we're all into the same stuff—Diamond Head, Budgie... Metallica came along and started playing everywhere.

Prior to Burton's joining, Metallica had recorded the No Life 'Til Leather *demo, which featured much of the material that would eventually comprise* Kill 'Em All. *The demo becomes a hot item on the underground tape-trading circuit.*

HOLT The tape-trading scene was how we all got heard. You would record a demo and the traders would circulate it all over the world—to all the fans, the magazines and the independent record labels.

KING Metallica's demo got passed around, big time. We all had that.

SCOTT IAN (Anthrax guitarist) When I heard *No Life 'Til Leather* I immediately thought, Wow, here's some guys from the other side of the country that are doing the same thing we're doing; they're just a little better at it right now. I remember being there the day Jonny Z [*Jon Zazula, owner of New Jersey record store Rock N' Roll Heaven and founder of indie label Megaforce Records*] got it in the mail. He put it on, and I was like, "That's fucking killer! Who are these guys?" Jonny told me, "They're called Metallica, and I'm bringing them to New York. Somehow we're gonna make a record."

JONNY Z We hustled together $1,500 for them to rent a van to come out to the East Coast and play some shows.

Metallica set up shop at the Music Building in Queens, New York, where Anthrax practice as well. The band lives and rehearses at the space and plays its first East Coast gigs.

IAN Metallica were opening for Vandenberg [*the group guitarist Adrian Vandenberg led prior to joining Whitesnake*] at L'amour in Brooklyn, and we were all down there in the afternoon, waiting for them to soundcheck. Mustaine was already shitfaced by 3:30, and he was yelling at Adrian Vandenberg, "Get the fuck off the stage! You suck!" And we were all like, "What the *fuck*, dude? *Shhhh!*"

SLAGEL Everybody liked to drink back then and have a good time, but Dave could go much further over the line than anyone else would, and you could see that sooner or later that was going to be a problem.

IAN I showed up at the Music Building for band practice one day, and Cliff was outside smoking a cigarette. He told me they had just kicked Dave out of the band. The other guys said, "We had known we were gonna do it for weeks now. We woke him up this morning, and he was so drunk and hungover that before he could even realize what was going on we got him out of here." I asked them what they were going to do, and they said they already had another guy on his way into town. His name was Kirk Hammett, and he was the guitar player in Exodus.

KIRK HAMMETT I was familiar with Metallica's music before I joined the band. I had the *No Life 'Til Leather* demo, and my friends and I listened to it quite a bit. It was what everyone in the San Francisco underground metal scene was listening to in 1982. Plus, Exodus played with Metallica pretty often in San Francisco. The first time I spoke to Lars was after they had just finished a set and I said, "Thanks for letting us play. I really like you guys." He said, "Yeah, yeah, cool, cool," but as I was talking to him, he started taking his stage clothes off, and before I knew it he was just completely naked in front of me, and I was just shocked. I said to myself, Oh, he's European. Europeans do stuff like this.

LARS ULRICH I remember the first time I heard Kirk. He had a feel that very few young players have—very rooted in European metal. It was really nice to hear an American guy who didn't play like Eddie Van Halen.

KILL 'EM ALL

In the spring of 1983, Metallica travel to Music America Studios in Rochester, New York, to record their debut album, Kill 'Em All, *with producer Paul Curcio.*

HAMMETT We totally trashed the place. I felt bad. But it's four guys, you know? There was carpet in every single room, and we drank pretty much 24 hours a day back then. So you can imagine how that turned out. Moist places shouldn't have rugs.

ULRICH The actual studio was in the basement of this huge old colonial-type of clubhouse. On the second floor there was a huge ballroom; perfect for getting a good drum sound. The problem was the place was fucking haunted. My cymbals would start spinning for no reason. Shit like that. It was scary.

HETFIELD Occasionally we put guitar and bass amps in the [*ballroom*] for ambience. I remember Cliff being in that room with all his amps and his headphones on while he recorded "(Anesthesia) Pulling Teeth," his bass solo. He literally was just standing in front of his amps.

HAMMETT The guitar stuff was recorded through James' magical, mythical Marshall. He had it modified by some guy in L.A. who used to work on Eddie Van Halen's gear. I used it too, because we didn't have much equipment back then. I also used a wah pedal and a Boss Super Distortion. James played his white Flying V and I used my black Flying V. Those were the only guitars we had.

Hammett, who has only been in the band a few months, still has to contend with the looming presence of Dave Mustaine, who had written many of the riffs and solos to the songs.

HAMMETT Jonny Z said, "You know, you have to play Dave's solos." I said, "No, I don't really want to play Dave's solos." He said, "Why don't you play the opening to every solo, so that people think you're going to play Dave's solos, and then you can go somewhere else with them." And that's exactly what I did. As a 20-year-old kid, put in a position like that, you don't want to rock the boat too much—especially being the new guy. So I took the first four bars of most of the solos and changed them.

HETFIELD Dave brought the song "The Four Horsemen" over from one of his other bands. Back then it was called "The Mechanix." After he left Metallica, we kind of fixed the song up. The lyrics he used were pretty silly.

Kill 'Em All *is released on July 25, 1983, on Megaforce. Though the first wave of thrash bands, including Exodus, Slayer, Anthrax and Overkill, are up and running, Metallica are the first act to record and release a full-length vinyl album.*

HETFIELD It was Cliff who named the album. Originally we were supposed to call it "Metal Up Your Ass." We got a phone call from our manager telling us half the record outlets wouldn't carry the album if it was called that. Cliff said, "You know what? Fuck those fuckers, man. We should just kill 'em all."

HAMMETT After we recorded the album and we came back to the Bay Area, there seemed to be 10 or 12 newer bands that were playing faster, really aggressive beats.

DAVE ELLEFSON (former Megadeth bassist) I remember early on Dave [*Mustaine*] got a fan letter from some kid in the Bay Area who wrote, "Can't wait to hear your new stuff. Hope it's faster than Metallica." We went to rehearsal the next day and everything jumped up 50 beats per minute!

HAMMETT Part of the reason why we would play so fast is because we were just nervous. As a young musician, when I was nervous I had a tendency to speed things up. Joining Metallica, I thought, This is great, because it can never be too fast.

HETFIELD Lars was always nervous onstage, so he'd play faster and faster. Nobody wanted to wimp out and tell him. We just figured, Hell, we'll just play fast too, and that's what we did on the record.

HAMMETT I would have been happy selling [*a few*] copies and being able to do a club tour across the States. To me, that was success. Then when we found out we were actually going to go to Europe and play shows there for the first time I thought, Oh my God, that's totally unexpected. For James and Cliff and myself, we had never been outside the United States. It was all very inspiring, because there were more possibilities out there than we imagined at the onset.

IAN Jonny Z had been trying to land Metallica a deal, and all the guys at the big labels would put their fingers in their ears when he played them the album. They were clueless. But when they saw how many copies Jonny sold, they realized, Wow, there's thousands of kids out there who are into this shit.

JONNY Z We printed up 1,500 copies, and they went in five seconds. We printed another 3,500, and they went in a week. We just kept on building and building, and then Elektra picked them up for *Ride the Lightning*.

RIDE THE LIGHTNING

After completing a European tour opening for Venom in early 1984, Metallica travel to Sweet Silence Studios in Copenhagen, Denmark, to record their second album, with producer Flemming Rasmussen. The result, Ride the Lightning, *is issued on Megaforce on July 27. A few months later, after a gig in New York City, the band is signed by Elektra, making them the first thrash metal act to be picked up by a major label. Elektra then reissues* Ride the Lightning *in the fall of 1984.*

ULRICH Cliff was responsible for a lot of the things that happened between *Kill 'Em All* and *Ride the Lightning*. He really exposed James and I to a whole new musical horizon of harmonies and melodies. [*Our*] whole way of writing songs together was very much shaped around Cliff's musical input.

HETFIELD Touring definitely made us a little more worldly. We started to see other things that were going on in the world. And that's when more of the punk-oriented, opinionated kind of thoughts began to appear in our lyrics. And actually having to sit down and write an album made a difference, because *Kill 'Em All* was just songs we had been playing in clubs for the two years before we recorded it.

HAMMETT I tracked the whole album with Marshall amps and my Gibson Flying V, and by then James had his Gibson Explorer.

HETFIELD That whole album was a real huge step for us. "Creeping Death" was our first big, chanting, gang-vocal thing. There was almost some production value to it!

HAMMETT When we did the crunchy "Die by my hand" breakdown in the middle, we sat in the control room after we did the gang vocals, and everyone was just going nuts!

In addition to thrashy cuts like "Creeping Death," "Fight Fire with Fire" and "For Whom the Bell Tolls," the album features the song "Fade to Black," which many consider the first thrash-metal ballad.

SLAGEL Metallica really pushed the boundaries with "Fade to Black." That was the first time any of the bands tried something like that. I remember some of their hardcore fans accused them of selling out with that song, but it's pretty obvious that it's just a great, extremely well-written tune.

HETFIELD It's a suicide song, and we got a lot of flack for it; kids were killing themselves because of the song. But we also got hundreds and hundreds of letters from kids telling us how they related to the song and that it made them feel better. It was also pretty much our first ballad, so it was challenging, and we knew it would freak people out.

HAMMETT For the extended solo at the end I wasn't sure what to play. We had been in Denmark for five or six months, and I was getting really homesick. Since it was a somber song and we were all bummed out anyway, I thought of some depressing things when I did the solo— and it really helped! When that was finished, I went back and did the clean guitar parts behind the verse. James played an arpeggiated figure while I arpeggiated three-note chords. We ended up getting a very Dire Straits–type of sound.

HETFIELD Bands like Exodus and Slayer don't do ballads, but they've stuck themselves in that position, which is something we've never wanted to do. Limiting yourself to please your audience is bullshit.

With the support of Elektra, Metallica begin to make inroads to the mainstream. Throughout 1984 and 1985 the band tours the world, embarking on the Bang the Head That Doesn't Bang tour across Europe and playing the U.S. with W.A.S.P. and Armored Saint. In August of 1985, Metallica appear at the Day on the Green festival in Oakland, California, where they perform before an audience of 60,000. That same month, they play to more than 70,000 at the Monsters of Rock festival in Donington, England, where they're sandwiched on the bill between Ratt and Bon Jovi.

HETFIELD (onstage at Monsters of Rock) If you came here to see spandex, eye makeup, and the words "Oh baby" in every fuckin' song, this ain't the fuckin' band.

MASTER OF PUPPETS

After touring for much of the year, Metallica returns to Sweet Silence Studios in September 1985, to begin work on their third album, Master of Puppets, *again with Flemming Rasmussen at the helm.*

HAMMETT By that point, we had been playing together for a few years. We'd toured a ton; we knew each other musically and personally; everybody was contributing amazing ideas, and it was just a culmination of all the right spots and all the right notes at the right time. Maybe the planets were aligned or something, I don't know, but that's what it felt like.

HETFIELD We started getting into the longer, more orchestrated songs. It was more of a challenge to write a long song that didn't seem long.

HAMMETT I'll tell you how the main [*descending*] riff to "Master of Puppets" came about. On the *Ride the Lightning* tour, James would always play the riff in the dressing room, but on the D string, and I'd play it simultaneously on the G string as a parallel-fourths harmony line. It sounded really dorky and funny. Then one day at rehearsal, James said, "Let me show you this really heavy song intro," and proceeded to play that exact riff on the low E string. I said, "Ah, so you finally found a use for that dorky little thing!" It's anything but dorky now.

HETFIELD The riff for the title track was pretty messy—constantly moving. But it works good live. People love to scream *Master!* a couple of times.

HAMMETT I used a Mesa/Boogie Mark II-C head and my Jackson Randy Rhoads V on that song. When you listen to the solo, there's this weird sound right after the mellow part where it sounds like I'm hitting a super high note, like I'm fretting the string against the pickup. What happened was, I accidentally pulled the string off the fretboard, and it fretted out on the side of the neck! I heard it back and was like, "That's brilliant! We've gotta keep that!" Of course, I've never been able to reproduce it since.

Master of Puppets *is released on March 3, 1986. In addition to the epic title track, the album features incredibly aggressive material like "Battery," "Damage, Inc." and "Disposable Heroes," as well as a second ballad, "Welcome Home (Sanitarium)."*

Sticker that appeared on the cover of early pressings of Master of Puppets: "The only track you probably won't want to play is 'Damage, Inc.' due to the multiple use of the infamous 'F' word. Otherwise, there aren't any 'Shits,' 'Fucks,' 'Pisses,' 'Cunts,' 'Motherfuckers,' or 'Cocksuckers' anywhere on this record."

HETFIELD The idea for "Welcome Home (Sanitarium)" came from the movie *One Flew Over the Cuckoo's Nest.* "Fade to Black" worked well, and we wanted to have another slow, clean, picking type of song, this time with a chorus. I had trouble singing that chorus—it's really high. And the riff for the song was lifted from some other band, who shall remain anonymous.

Master of Puppets peaks at Number 29 on the Billboard album chart, and within a few months of its release sells more than 500,000 copies. With no help from radio or MTV, Metallica earn their first Gold-certified album. The band receives a large amount of main-stream exposure from their opening slot on Ozzy Osbourne's tour in support of his Ultimate Sin album.

HAMMETT Going on the Ozzy tour really made a difference, because all of a sudden we were playing *Master of Puppets* to a pretty mainstream audience. Your typical Ozzy fan might not have gotten Metallica, but two or three years later, they were all saying, "Yeah, I saw Metallica with Ozzy, and they blew him away!" We converted people night after night. Suddenly we were selling albums, and a lot of it had to do with playing our asses off, putting on a great show, just bringing the music to the people in that way, because radio wasn't having us.

In the fall of '86, Metallica embark on the European leg of the Damage, Inc. tour, with Anthrax supporting.

DAN SPITZ (Anthrax guitarist) The aura each night when they got on-stage was incredible. I imagine Led Zeppelin and Black Sabbath had that same vibe. Seeing Metallica back then, you just knew something big was about to happen. *Master of Puppets* was the changing of the guard.

On September 27, while en route to a gig in Copenhagen, Metallica's tour bus skids off the road near Dorarp, Sweden, and flips over several times. Cliff Burton, asleep in his bunk, is thrown through a window. The bus falls on top of him, killing him instantly. He was 24 years old.

HETFIELD I saw the bus lying right on him. I saw his legs sticking out. I went to pieces. The driver tried to take Cliff's blanket to give that to someone else. I just screamed, "Fuck that!" I wanted to kill the guy. I didn't know if he was drunk or if the bus had skidded on ice. All I knew was Cliff was dead.

HAMMETT A part of Metallica was lost forever when he died.

HETFIELD The only thing I could think was: The band? No way! There ain't no band. The band is not the band right now. It's just three guys.

IAN It was a terrible time. You just don't imagine something like that happening to one of your friends, especially when you're on tour, because there's this feeling of invincibility. But I know that the rest of Metallica never considered ending the band. Their attitude was, Why would we stop? That's the last thing Cliff would want us to do.

A few weeks after Burton's funeral, Hetfield, Ulrich and Hammett begin auditioning bass players. They eventually settle on 23-year-old Flotsam and Jetsam bassist Jason Newsted.

ULRICH We did about 60 people in one week. And we decided that we wanted to ask four back. Jason was second of the four. We played all day, and then went out for a meal. And then we went for the big test, which was the drink test. Somehow, I swear it wasn't planned, me, Kirk and James ended up in the toilet together, pissing. So we're standing there at three in the morning, out of our faces, all of us in a line, not saying anything. And I just said without looking at anybody, "That's him, right?" And the other guys said, "Yeah, that's him." And that was it.

JASON NEWSTED When I came into Metallica, I had to do justice to Cliff's work, but I also had to put my own signature on it. No one could be Cliff Burton; Cliff Burton was the Jimi Hendrix of bass. I had to practice, practice, practice to get anywhere close to where he was.

HOLT After all these years, anyone who plays bass in Metallica is still filling Cliff Burton's shoes. There was nobody like him.

With Newsted onboard, Metallica head back out to the road, touring America and Europe with Metal Church, and ending with three shows as part of the Monsters of Rock festival. In the summer of 1987, they return to L.A. and record The $5.98 E.P.: Garage Days Re-Revisited. *The set features covers of songs by Metallica favorites the Misfits, Budgie and NWOBHM legends Diamond Head.*

HAMMETT We did that EP for the fans, just for fun, and Elektra loved it and released it. All the lead parts flowed really quickly; I did them in two nights. That was when I first started using ESP guitars with EMG pickups.

HETFIELD We were still dealing with Cliff's death, and Q-Prime, our management, was telling us to jump right back into it and start playing again. I guess we kind of mourned through music and doing the cover songs on that album.

...AND JUSTICE FOR ALL

In January 1988, Metallica reconvene with producer Flemming Rasmussen, this time at One On One Studios in Los Angeles, to begin work on their fourth full-length album. Titled ...And Justice for All, *the effort is the most progressive and technically challenging in the band's catalog, boasting just nine songs for a combined length of more than one hour.*

HAMMETT Things changed after Cliff's death. Even our sound changed. On *Justice*, we kind of fell prey to that whole virtuosic, late-

Eighties thing that was happening. All of a sudden, everyone wanted to be progressive and show off their abilities. Somehow, just playing fast and heavy took a backseat to that.

HETFIELD Sometimes we look back at some of our material and wonder how—or *why*—we ever came up with certain parts. There was a lot of urgency to that material, but a lot of it was just wank—just us showing off. But that's where we were at that time.

Though the album is Newsted's first full-length effort with Metallica, his bass parts are almost completely inaudible on the finished product. This is widely believed to be the result of the rest of the band's "hazing" of the bassist, though they deny the charge.

HETFIELD The bass was obscured for two reasons. First, Jason tended to double my rhythm guitar parts, so it was hard to tell where my guitar started and his bass left off. Also, my tone on *Justice* was very scooped—all lows and highs, with very little midrange. When my rhythm parts were placed in the mix, my guitar sound ate up all the lower frequencies. Jason and I were always battling for the same space in the mix.

NEWSTED I can't explain how much grief I dealt with—and still deal with—over that record.

HAMMETT There was a lot of anguish after Cliff died, and basically Jason was the punching bag. We vented so much on him, and it wasn't really fair.

...And Justice for All is released on September 6, 1988, and becomes Metallica's biggest album to date. It is also their mainstream breakthrough. This is in large part due to the success of the song "One," for which the band films its first music video. In the video, Hetfield's

*dark lyrics are set against disturbing images from the 1971 film adaptation of Dalton Trumbo's antiwar novel, **Johnny Got His Gun**.*

HETFIELD We'd never done a video until then because we'd never been asked to. We certainly didn't want to get to the position where we had to beg MTV to play one of our videos. Our fans were calling them up and asking for our videos to be played. MTV were like, Who the hell are Metallica? But they ended up asking us to make a video. So we finally did one, and we did it our way. And, of course, it was incredibly disturbing.

HAMMETT I knew we were on to a good thing when I saw "One" on MTV at, like, 11:30 in the evening. I watched it, and afterward the VJ came on and said, "Wow, that's a real bowl of rainbows!"

*In the wake of the album's massive success—it peaks at Number Six on the **Billboard** album chart, and is certified Platinum in less than three months—Metallica embark on Damaged Justice, their first headlining arena tour, which takes them around the world and stretches on for more than a year. "One" is also nominated for a Grammy—the first year the Recording Academy offers the Best Hard Rock/Metal Performance category—but the band loses to Jethro Tull, a band whose music is neither hard rock nor metal.*

ULRICH I'd be lying if I didn't tell you I was disappointed. Human nature is that you'd rather win than lose, but Jethro Tull walking away with it makes a huge mockery of the intentions of the event.

Sticker on the cover of subsequent copies of ...And Justice for All: "Grammy Award LOSERS."

THE BLACK ALBUM

After completing the Damaged Justice tour, Metallica return to One On One Studios in October 1990 to record their fifth studio album. The music they write and record largely eschews their thrash metal roots in favor of a decidedly more commercial sound with slower tempos, simpler guitar riffs and shorter, more accessible songs. James Hetfield's vocals are more melodic as well. This change in sound is credited by many to the influence of producer Bob Rock, best known for his work with radio-friendly acts like Bon Jovi and Mötley Crüe.

HETFIELD People will be saying Bob [*Rock*] made Metallica sound like Bon Jovi. They don't realize that no one screws with us, except us.

ULRICH One thing that Bob should be given total credit for is making James comfortable enough to take that guard down and really sing. We've always thought of ourselves as Big Bad Metallica, but Bob taught us a new word none of us had ever heard before: "soulful."

HETFIELD Radio airplay wasn't the whole idea behind our writing shorter songs. It seemed to us that we had pretty much done the longer song format to death. We have one song that has just two riffs in it, which is pretty amazing. It only takes two minutes to get the point across.

By the time the new album is released, on August 13, 1991, Metallica have been in the studio for close to a year, and the cost of the production reaches one million dollars. They choose to title the record Metallica, though due to its stark cover image—a coiled snake against a black background—it comes to be known as the Black Album.

NEWSTED It took us a long time to think up that title. I guess we could have just called it "Five" or named it after one of the songs. We wanted to keep it simple.

ULRICH The songs aren't so busy, and Kirk's guitar playing fits in well when he plays with the laid-back drums. James and I tried to set things up that were easier for Kirk to solo over. Some of the things on *Justice* got a little out of hand. Then it was, "Okay, Kirk, solo over this!" And it would be the most sideways, difficult thing.

NEWSTED The bass sound is much weightier. I tried to create a real rhythm section rather than a one-dimensional sound. It comes down to the music—making it a real rhythm section for once, and letting the guitars do their work. I'm glad the rest of the band could tell me that that's what was needed.

HETFIELD What we really wanted was a live feel. In the past, Lars and I constructed the rhythm parts without Kirk and Jason. This time I wanted to try playing as a band unit in the studio. It lightens things up and you get more of a vibe.

HAMMETT I used a Bradshaw preamp for the lows and mids and a couple of Marshalls for the nice clean highs. We EQ'd it through the board a little bit, and it worked out great. And I used two guitars—a Strat-style ESP with two EMG [*pickups*] and an '89 Les Paul Deluxe with two EMGs.

HETFIELD We tried a bunch of amps, but I ended up using the same Mesa/Boogie Mark II Simul Class that I've used on the last three albums. My primary guitar was my ESP Explorer with EMGs, but I also used a Telecaster, a Gretsch White Falcon with a Bigsby and a Guild 12-string.

The album's lead-off track, "Enter Sandman," is propelled by a simple and hooky riff and a huge, sing-along chorus. It becomes a worldwide smash hit.

HETFIELD I can remember when I wrote the lyrics to "Enter Sandman," Bob Rock and Lars came to me and said, "These aren't as good as they could be." And that pissed me off so much. I was like, "Fuck you! I'm the writer here!" That was the first challenge from someone else, and it made me work harder.

HAMMETT I think the time has come to reveal where I actually got the guitar lick before the breakdown in "Enter Sandman": It's from "Magic Man," by Heart, but I didn't get it from Heart's version; I got it from a cut off Ice-T's *Power* album, where he sampled it. I heard that and thought, I have to snake this!

Mainstream music fans wholeheartedly embrace the new, friendlier Metallica. The Black Album enters the **Billboard** *album chart at Number One and sells 600,000 copies in its first week of release. In addition to "Enter Sandman," the record spawns five more hit singles, including "The Unforgiven," "Wherever I May Roam" and the acoustic ballad "Nothing Else Matters." The album has since sold more than 22 million copies worldwide.*

ULRICH You think one day some fucker's going to tell you, "You have a Number One record in America" and the whole world will ejaculate. I stood there in my hotel room, and there was this fax that said, 'You're Number One.' And it was like, Well, okay. It was just another fucking fax from the office.

BEYOND THE BLACK

In October 1991, Metallica embark on the Wherever We May Roam tour. They stay on the road for close to three years, in the process becoming one of the biggest touring and recording acts in the world. Over the next decade the band releases a series of albums—Load, ReLoad, St. Anger—on which they continually reinvent their sound (and image), gaining—and losing—fans in the process. In 2001, Jason Newsted leaves Metallica due to strained relations with the rest of the band, in particular James Hetfield. In 2003 he is replaced by ex–Suicidal Tendencies and Ozzy Osbourne bassist Robert Trujillo, who joins prior to the tour in support of St. Anger. In September 2008, Metallica release their ninth studio album, **Death Magnetic.** *To date they've sold more than 90 million records worldwide, and remain one of the most influential and successful bands in hard rock and heavy metal.*

HAMMETT I think Metallica have a lot more to say. We're the type of band that likes to experiment. We don't like to stay in one spot for too long; all the albums after the Black Album prove that. We're not afraid to take artistic risks, even at the cost of pissing off our audience and our friends.

HETFIELD The cool thing about Metallica is that there's always a new generation of angry young men who latch onto *Kill 'Em All* and know what I'm talking about. And maybe they grow up with the rest of the records. We've never been about creating some fantasy world with our records; we're just documenting where we're at at the time. There's always going to be youth on the planet, and whether they can relate to that or not, I don't know. But every time I look out in the crowd and see some kids battling it out in the middle of the mosh pit, I'm like, "Yeah, I was there, man."

HAMMETT We want to get out there and show people how strong Metallica is. It's not a mask and it's not bullshit. We feel really good about being us right now, and here we are. Now, see if you can hang on.

REPRINTED FROM *GUITAR WORLD*, FEBRUARY 2008

[3]

"Joining Metallica, I just thought,
This is great, because
it can never be too fast."
—KIRK HAMMETT

HAMMER TIME

With their 1983 debut, *Kill 'Em All*,
Metallica served notice that thrash had arrived
in all its pummeling glory. On the album's
25th anniversary, Kirk Hammett reveals the story
behind the making of a metal milestone.

BY ALAN DI PERNA

ETALLICA HAVE NEVER DONE anything the easy way. On the eve of recording their first album, *Kill 'Em All*, these raging stepchildren of the New Wave of British Heavy Metal fired their lead guitarist Dave Mustaine after a rather savage fistfight with James Hetfield, brought about when Hetfield allegedly accused Mustaine of kicking his dog. Never mind that the band were holed up in a charmless house on the mean streets of Jamaica, Queens, 3,000 miles from home, or that it was the middle of a January cold snap; never mind that Mustaine had cowritten four of the songs destined for the album, for which Metallica had already booked studio time. Then, as now, the nexus of James Hetfield and drummer Lars Ulrich made up Metallica's power base. Mustaine was out. There would be no turning back.

Within hours of the guitarist's dismissal, Ulrich was on the phone and negotiating an audition with Kirk Hammett, the 20-year-old guitarist from Exodus, one of San Francisco's preeminent thrash metal bands. Armed with a copy of Metallica's *No Life 'Til Leather* demo, Hammett learned their songs over a one-week period, then hopped a flight to New York, made for the band's rehearsal space and plugged in his Flying V within hours of landing. Less than a month later, Metallica's "Four Horsemen"—Hetfield, Hammett, Ulrich and original bassist Cliff Burton—were intact and tracking 12 roiling songs of complex savagery and rage, creating a bludgeoning opus of fast, crude and rude songs that would signal the birth of American heavy metal and kick off a 25-year hegemony that hasn't abated yet.

In this exclusive interview, *Guitar World* probes Kirk Hammett's memory to learn what happened during those seminal three weeks in Rochester, New York, when *Kill 'Em All* was recorded. Kirk explains how he staked his claim in Mustaine territory, why Metallica played so fast and why Cliff Burton always kept a hammer in his pocket—an image immortalized on the cover of *Kill 'Em All*.

GUITAR WORLD You joined Metallica only a month before they recorded *Kill 'Em All*—how long did it take you to learn the songs and write solos for them?

KIRK HAMMETT I was familiar with Metallica's music before I joined the band. I had the *No Life 'Til Leather* demo, and me and my friends listened to it quite a bit. It was what everyone in the San Francisco underground metal scene was listening to in 1982.

GW Didn't you also play on the same bills as Metallica?

HAMMETT Exodus played with Metallica quite a bit. So I knew the songs. When I got the phone call asking if I wanted to try out for the band, I already had the demo, I could already play one or two of the riffs, and I was familiar with that style of music, more so than your guy who grew up just listening to Aerosmith, Van Halen and Led Zeppelin. I listened to the Scorpions, Motörhead, UFO, Angel Witch, Tigers of Pan Tang, Iron Maiden, Judas Priest. I learned all the songs in about a week. When I flew out there and started playing with those guys, they instantly loved what I was doing.

"Cliff was such an original thinker, and he had so much confidence."
—*HAMMETT*

GW What were your initial impressions of James and Lars?

HAMMETT I had met James and Lars when I was in Exodus and we played with them. I remember thinking James was really quiet and really shy and mellow, and wondering how can this shy, mellow guy just be the screaming banshee that I see onstage there? I was struck by the dichotomy. The more I got to know him, the more I thought he's just a really cool guy, really clever. We had similar family upbringings, and he was a great guitar player who's into a lot of the same things I was into, musically. And it was fun hanging out with him. James liked to wrestle when he was drunk, though. So whenever we were drunk, things would start getting physical, and I learned early on that if James reached that point where he was just wanting to wrestle, I would make sure there was a bunch of people in between him and I.

GW What about Lars?

HAMMETT The first time I spoke to him was when Exodus played with Metallica. They had just finished playing their set and I said to him, "Thanks a lot for letting us play. I really like you guys. I can hear the influence of the New Wave of British Heavy Metal bands in your sound." "Yeah, yeah, cool, cool," he said, but as I was talking to him, he started taking his stage clothes off, and before I knew it he was completely naked in front of me, and I was just shocked. I said to myself, "Oh, he's European. Europeans do stuff like this." But my eyes never left his eyes. I wasn't going to step back, check him out or anything like that. But I was slightly shocked and mortified by his undressing.

GW Tell me about Cliff Burton.

HAMMETT As I said earlier, Cliff was such an original thinker, and he had so much confidence. He was so much his own person. He wasn't going to take shit from anyone and he always let everyone know that. It was Cliff who named the album. Originally we were supposed to call the album "Metal Up Your Ass." We got a phone call from our manager telling us half the record outlets wouldn't carry the album if it's called that because the name was obscene. We were pissed off, but we knew we had to think up a new name. We were walking from the place we were staying to the photographer's studio to shoot the portrait on the back cover and thinking about names for the album, and Cliff said, "You know what? Fuck those fuckers, man, those fucking record outlet people. Just, we should just kill 'em all." Someone, I can't remember who, said, "That's it! That's what we should call the album, *Kill 'Em All*. We all agreed and that's how the album was named.

GW Let's get back to that initial phone call when they asked you to audition, did you immediately go to the studio in Rochester?

HAMMETT No, we went to Jamaica, Queens. There was a house that they were living in in a pretty scary part of town.

GW Were you anxious?

HAMMETT No. I had a week to learn the songs. At the end of that week I flew out, met those guys, and I had a week to rehearse with them, and then we started playing shows all over the Tri-State area. Every show just kept on getting better and better. When it came time to go into the studio, Johnny Z, our manager said, "You know you have to play Dave's solos." "No, I don't really want to play Dave's solos." I said. "Then why don't you take the opening to every single solo, so that people think that they're Dave's solos and then you can go somewhere else with them," he said. "Okay. I'll do that," I told him. As a 20-year-old kid, put in a position like that, you don't want to rock the boat too much, especially being the new kid in town—the fresh guy. So I said, "Sure." That's exactly what I did. I took the first four bars of most of the solos and changed them. When I changed them it was always for the better and everyone liked it.

GW How was playing with Metallica different than Exodus?

HAMMETT The musicianship was a lot better, in that there was more flexibility. It wasn't as one-dimensional. In Exodus it *was* a little bit one-dimensional. The bass player only wanted to play fast, the singer only wanted to sing a certain way, the drummer only wanted to play a certain way. Granted, we were all very young at the time. When I got into Metallica, it was just a better fit for my guitar style. The music was much more dynamic, the musicianship was much more dynamic. I felt that the riffs that I was writing could be put to much better use, because I wasn't the only one writing everything. When I was in Exodus I was writing everything.

GW Because you had formed that band, it must have been difficult to leave them.

HAMMETT Yeah, it was. A lot of my riffs ended up on *Bonded by Blood* [*Exodus' 1985 debut*] and I was just like, "whatever." You know, it's just a riff. My main focus was on Metallica, I wasn't going to go call up a lawyer and raise a big stink because some of my music is on *Bonded by Blood.*

GW Did you feel like you should have tried to keep one foot in Exodus?

HAMMETT No, I literally left Exodus and joined Metallica, all within about one week. Or more accurately, I left Exodus with the idea of going out to New York to audition for Metallica. They knew it—I had to tell them.

GW You fly out to New York, you audition, and within weeks you're recording an album with them. What do you remember about the actual recording?

HAMMETT The guitar stuff was recorded through James' magical, mythical Marshall. I used that mostly because we didn't have very much equipment back then. It was his first Marshall amp and he had it modified by some guy in L.A., the guy who used to modify Van Halen's guitars [*Jose Arrendondo*] and it just had a really great sound. I say magical mythical Marshall because it's not around anymore. Shortly after we did *Kill 'Em All*, we played some shows in Boston and someone broke into the equipment truck and stole that Marshall.

GW What guitars did you use during the recording?

HAMMETT We used the only guitars we had, which was James' white Flying V and my black Gibson Flying V that I used for the first four albums. I remember when we were tracking, so much time was spent tuning those guitars because we didn't have any backup guitars and we didn't have any techs or roadies in the studio so we pretty much had to change strings ourselves and tune up the guitars ourselves. But that was fine for us because that's what we were used to at that point.

We didn't have techs around us 24 hours a day like it seems like we do now when we're in the studio. Besides that, I just used a wah pedal and one of those Boss Super Distortions.

GW Is there any story behind your Gibson?

HAMMETT Yeah, it's a black Flying V that I got at Leo's Music in Oakland. I got a job washing dishes at the Mira Vista Country Club in Richmond, California, to pay for it. I worked there for about eight months and saved up enough money to buy that Flying V. And once I bought it, I quit. I was actually 15 and a half when I got the job.

GW Did you use any equipment from the studio?

HAMMETT At one point there was a break in the middle of "The Four Horsemen" where I thought it might sound good if there was like a whammy bar kind of fill, but I didn't have my guitar that usually had a whammy bar on it because I traded it away for a Marshall cabinet. And so we had to borrow one, and it wasn't even a proper whammy bar on it, like you know, a Fender Strat. The in-house producer knew the guitar player that used to be in a band called East West, and he had a Firebird that had a Bixby tremolo bar. I remember picking that up and trying to do some Strat-sound divebombs and thinking, This Bixby is not working for what I need it to do. No wonder Jimi Hendrix used Strats with tremolo units and not Gibsons with Bixby units, because it's just not the same.

GW What do you remember about the studio?

HAMMETT Well, I remember the studio [*Music America Studios, in Rochester, New York*] as being just like any other studio back in that day. It wasn't extravagant. It had a drum room with a piano in it, and the control room looked into the drum room. And then upstairs was this huge, huge loft space where they would occasionally record the drums.

GW Did you live there?

HAMMETT No, we lived at this place that belonged to one employee of the house and we totally thrashed it. I felt bad. We pretty much never washed the dishes. It's four guys, you know? There was carpet in every single room including the kitchen and the bathrooms, and we drank pretty much 24 hours a day back then. You can imagine how *that* turned out. Moist places everywhere. Places that were never meant to be moist. Rugs that never dried out. It was a mess.

GW So back to the studio.

HAMMETT There was a loft on the second floor and occasionally we put guitar and bass amps in there for ambience. I remember Cliff being in that room with all his amps and his headphones on, while he recorded "Pulling Teeth," his bass solo. He literally was just standing in front of his amps.

GW What did everyone say when Cliff said he wanted to put a bass solo on the record?

HAMMETT First of all it was a great piece of music. It was a stand-out piece of music. And Cliff was just so out there, and he was such an original thinker that we just thought, Wow, what a cool idea. Instead of an open guitar solo like Eddie Van Halen's "Eruption," we had this fantastic bass solo that Cliff wrote, so we thought, Why not put it on the album? It started off being a part of the live show—he would play it to give everyone else a break, and then the drums would come in and he would solo against the drums. He also had a big Morley wah pedal, which was unique, too. I remember at one point we tried to do overdubs in this big, empty space. Or actually Lars tried to do overdubs. One of them was the drum fills in "Hit the Lights." He had a couple of drum toms in the bathroom, which was this old tile bathroom, but it was just too bombastic. It didn't really fit. At the end of "Metal Militia" you hear this marching sound—that was Lars wearing heavy boots and marching up and down on this wooden floor and then miking it and multi-tracking it.

GW What do you remember about recording your parts?

HAMMETT Once all the rhythm tracks were done, I came in. Got a sound that was pretty much already there, using James' modified Marshall. We just tweaked a little here and there, and then I started recording the solos. I always record in the control room without cans on because listening to my guitar through headphones is just not the same as just listening to it through either a speaker cabinet or through monitors. It's too close to my eardrums. I need space in between what's coming out of the speaker and my ears.

GW What was the schedule?

HAMMETT We would work from the afternoon until about 11 or 12 or so at night. And then we would pretty much start drinking afterward. I remember that we had three weeks to track everything. I took about a week to do all my guitar solos. I wasn't spending the entire day doing guitar solos. It was five or six hours of doing guitar solos and then we'd go to something else. When everything was recorded, the engineer and the producer decided that they wanted to mix the album themselves, then pretty much locked us out of the studio while they were mixing it. They added all these weird delays and reverb and these things that we wouldn't have done. That's why there's such a drastic sonic difference between *Kill 'Em All* and *Ride the Lightning*. There are also things that had been recorded that

"I remember when it came out, it was the achievement of our lives. Our first album."

we would have liked to have fixed or re-recorded, but we couldn't because we just basically ran out of time.

GW I read somewhere that only 1500 copies were initially printed?

HAMMETT There was a very, very low print run at first. I think it was more like 15,000. I want to say like 15- to 30,000 at the beginning. I remember when it came out, it was the achievement of our lives. Our first album. We could hold it and show people and go, "Hey, look, we made an album. We're on vinyl." It was a great feeling.

GW Did you have the awareness that this album would be turning hard music on its head?

HAMMETT We knew that Metallica as a band was like no other band out there. We knew we were onto something different, but me personally, I did not think that we would hit the heights that we were going to hit. I was happy selling like, you know, 20– to 30,000 copies and being able to do a club tour across the States. That to me was success. Then when we found out that we were actually going to go to Europe and play shows there for the first time, I thought, Oh my God. That's totally unexpected. For James and Cliff and myself, we had never been out of the United States, and so that was quite a landmark as well. We were definitely on a mission for world domination. When we went over to Europe and started playing these shows in front of like audiences of two- to 3,000 people, which was like phenomenal for us at the beginning, we started to get a perspective on how things could be, and how we could steer this into something really, really substantial and important and influential. That we could turn this into a career. It was all just very inspiring because there were more possibilities out there than we really, truly imagined at the onset.

GW Which solo on the record are you most proud of?

HAMMETT "The Four Horsemen," definitely. I recorded one solo and then I thought, I can do that better, and I recorded a second solo. I wasn't in love with that one either, so I said to the engineer, "Let's hear that second solo back." That's when I found out that he didn't mute the first solo, so both solos played the same time. When I heard it I said, "Wow, that's a cool effect." Cliff Burton was standing right there and said, "That's fantastic. That's like Tony Iommi." I thought it was pretty cool, too, because I was going in and out of harmony with myself. I remember playing it for the other guys and they just looked at me and said, "That's fantastic, let's leave it the way it is." I still like that solo a lot. That was one of the cooler guitar solos for me because it was a solo that wasn't on the demo. We added that middle section right before we went into the studio.

GW Did you feel that you were staking your claim to that song, and making it yours instead of Dave Mustaine's?

HAMMETT Totally. I would agree 100 percent.

GW Did they give you any instructions on what to play or how to play the things from the demos?

HAMMETT No, not really. The only instruction was, if I was playing a bad note in a riff or something. "It's not F, it's F♯."

GW Other than "The Four Horsemen," what other tracks did you like.

HAMMETT I really like "No Remorse" and "Phantom Lord." And "Seek and Destroy," even though there are some out-of-tune bends. There're a couple notes that are out of tune. And that's what I was talking about earlier, that I would have loved to have had the time to fix it but we didn't have time.

GW How critical were you of your own performance?

HAMMETT I remember getting the test pressing and listening to it and thinking, Oh my God, no one can hear this! This is not good enough! I remember just freaking out, but keeping it to myself, thinking, God, I wish I could play as well as Jimmy Page played on the first Zeppelin album. After I listened to it for about two or three weeks, I thought, This is me. I can't compare myself to some other musician, I just have to be myself and let people hear me. Then I was over it, and it was fine.

GW Which of the songs do you think stand the test of time?

HAMMETT I think from start to finish it's a complete package. It's young, raw, obnoxious, loud, fast, energetic and inspirational, and everything in between.

GW The reviews of *Kill 'Em All* would mention things like "Metallica has created a new kind of metal" or "it was a creative rebirth of hard rock"? You agree?

HAMMETT I think that we were onto a sound that was unique because there were no hard rock or heavy metal albums up to that point that sounded like *Kill 'Em All*, in terms of intensity, speed and aggression. I really thought that we had some really great riffs that were as good as any riffs on a Judas Priest or Iron Maiden album, which were considered the heaviest stuff at that day. I thought that this was basically different from all that. It had elements of that in our sound, definitely, but there were certain ingredients in our mix—we had great melodies going on. Just really catchy stuff. We had stuff that sounded really, really great after a six-pack of beer.

GW It's more commonly said that Metallica forged its identity with your next album, *Ride the Lightning*, with some of the slower, intro-spective songs on it like "Fade to Black." Is that accurate or was it there from the beginning?

HAMMETT I definitely thought we did it on *Kill 'Em All*. We were just very inspired back then. We were young, we were hungry. We had a lot to say—we had a lot of ideas and a lot of youthful energy. Part of the reason why we would play so fast is because we were just nervous.

GW Really?

"**Cliff always had a hammer in his luggage,** and he would take it out occasionally and start destroying things."

HAMMETT It's the truth. I remember when I was a young musician, when I was really nervous I had a tendency to speed things up. Joining Metallica, I just thought, This is great, because it can never be too fast.

GW Did the specter of Dave Mustaine hang around the recordings, since he did co-write four of the songs?

HAMMETT Maybe for like the first three months or so. There were people going, where's Dave? Dave would make all these little comments about me onstage, but he didn't get a rebuttal from me. My whole attitude was I'm here to play guitar and not to be a cabaret act.

GW His debut album with Megadeth, *Killing Is My Business...And Business Is Good*, certainly borrowed from the title.

HAMMETT I could tell that he was just really angry at the band then, and really hateful toward the whole situation. But you know, my whole attitude was, let him run his mouth off. I'm not going to say anything. Because then he won't have any ammo to say anything about me.

GW What was the inspiration for the *Kill 'Em All* cover art?

HAMMETT Our manager told us because we were on a budget, we had to go with this photographer named Gary L. Heard. He's going to shoot the back cover portrait, and he's going to ask you for ideas for the front cover. At that point we were still wondering what the hell we were going to call the album. It was on the way to the photo shoot that we figured out that we were going to call it *Kill 'Em All*. We told the guy, and that's when Cliff Burton mentioned something about wanting there to be a bloody hammer on the cover—but then Cliff Burton carried a hammer with him everywhere he went.

GW He did?

HAMMETT He always had a hammer in his luggage, and he would take it out occasionally and start destroying things.

GW Like what?

HAMMETT Mostly dressing rooms. Or just like holes in the ground. In these shady nightclubs that we would play. We were going into the U.K. from France, and we got stopped at customs and they were going through our luggage. And all of a sudden this guy was going through Cliff's luggage, and he pulls out this hammer and looks at it, and looks at Cliff, and Cliff goes, "Hey, you never know when you might need it."

GW Did they take it away from him?

HAMMETT No, they didn't. It was a different world back then. They just took all the porn. We were a rock band, we all had porn with us, they took it. But they didn't take the hammer.

[4]

"We didn't set out to make
something that would
stand the test of time
20 years from now.
That wasn't on our radar at all."
—*KIRK HAMMETT*

MASTERPIECE

In the early Eighties Metallica were considered by their peers to be young, loud dickheads in cheap denim. With the release of their 1986 epic, *Master of Puppets*, they were declared geniuses—young, loud, dick-headed geniuses.

BY MICK WALL

KIRK HAMMETT CASTS HIS MIND back, sighs and, in a voice as quiet and flickering as a church candle, puts it like this: "I really felt that *Master of Puppets* was the album that defined that lineup—James, Lars, Cliff and I. Ninety-nine percent of it was conceived by the four of us. We had gotten to know each other's musical capabilities and temperaments over the three-year period we'd been together, and I could tell that it was really blossoming into something to be reckoned with. Every song we came up with was another great conception. Still, we never thought for a minute we'd still be talking about it 20 years later."

And with good reason. At the time of the album's release, in March 1986, Metallica were well outside the margins of mainstream rock.

Dee Snider of Twisted Sister, for whom Metallica opened in 1984, delivered the consensus opinion when he said the band members were "a nice bunch of kids" but there was "no way" they were ever going to make it. Consisting of Hammett, guitarist and singer James Hetfield, bassist Cliff Burton and drummer Lars Ulrich, Metallica were the sort of band that appealed to the self-obsessed skate-heads and thrash kids that wrote for and read the fanzines. As such, they and their music were good fun. The thought that they could be as significant as Iron Maiden and Judas Priest was laughable.

Master of Puppets changed those perceptions considerably. It was a pivotal release in every sense, for both Metallica and the rock scene they almost single-handedly transformed. Whether most mainstream rock critics actually understood the album or not—and most didn't—Metallica's place at the cutting edge of American rock was indisputable within months of the album's release.

Certainly, the sense that something major had occurred was palpable among the group's fans. Like the first water breathers to flop accidentally onto land, they'd discovered Metallica in 1983 via their first album, the injudiciously titled *Kill 'Em All*, and fallen in love with its unequivocal thrash classics like the hilariously straight-faced "The Four Horsemen" and the neck-aching "Whiplash." Its follow-up, 1984's *Ride the Lightning*, had drawn them deeper under the group's spell with the stunning range of its ambitious songs and dynamic arrangements that fused thrash with acoustic, pseudo-classical and straight-ahead rock. Nothing on the album typified these qualities as well as the album-closing instrumental, "The Call of Ktulu," and the evocative ballad "Fade to Black."

With *Master of Puppets*, Metallica took the bold developments of *Ride the Lightning* and cranked them up considerably. The diverse musical elements that had so startled listeners on the previous record were seamlessly integrated over the new album's length, giving Metallica's sound even greater power and presence. Even the lyrics seemed to benefit from the group's newfound focus. Thematically, the songs formed a treatise on power and fear, populated with religious and military figures, monsters and frail humans consumed by addiction and rage. Creatively, *Master of Puppets* was not so much a leap beyond *Ride the Lightning* as it was a refinement of that album's strengths. But as refinements go, it proved impossible to ignore.

For the group's hardcore base, this was both good and bad news. Though blown away by the album's focus and its polished production, they lamented not only that Metallica had begun not only to splinter from their thrash base but also to migrate from rock's fringe and toward its commercial borders.

But then, as Ulrich, their chief mouthpiece, told me at the time, "Metallica was never just a thrash band anyway. I accept that we had a lot to do with the way that whole scene took off. We were the first band to sound like that. But we never thought of ourselves as a 'thrash band.' We were always an American band with British and European metal influences." Metallica's members had always said as much in their interviews, he insisted. "It's just that until *Master of Puppets*, nobody took us seriously before."

It isn't hard to see why Metallica were roundly dismissed by the establishment in the years before *Master of Puppets*. Although they may not have been in the same league as Priest or Maiden, neither were they innovators of a new genre. As performers and songwriters, they were head and shoulders above their fellow Bay Area thrashers, but they came off as nerds in cheap denims, with tremble-tremble song titles like "For Whom the Bell Tolls" and "Seek and Destroy." With a few exceptions, their material was as ridiculously over the top as the moody "spaghetti western" music that preceded their shows. Apart from Burton, none of them had begun to assume the gravitas that would later characterize their public profile. Photos from this time are amateurishly silly: in one, Ulrich brandishes a pair of flaming drumsticks while pulling a suitably anguished face; in another, the group poses beside a giant vodka bottle stenciled with the word "Alcoholica."

It was at their shows, however, that one could see traces of Metallica's potential. Their downbeat image and sped-up sound were distinctly at odds with the prevailing, glammed-up rock fashions of the mid-Eighties, as epitomized by big hair and eyeliner acts like Mötley Crüe and Ratt. As a result, despite the dickhead image and ultrametal song titles, they quickly forged a reputation for themselves where it really mattered—on the road.

Yet, even that wasn't enough to soften the shock when, halfway through the *Ride the Lightning* tour, Metallica signed a megabuck eight-album deal with Elektra. Subsequently, when management team Q-Prime, home to chartbusters Def Leppard, picked up Metallica, it was evident to everyone that something was going on. But just what, no one seemed to know,

Certainly, there was no sense of history in the making when I visited the band in Copenhagen during the making of *Master of Puppets* in December 1985. Metallica had been recording the album at Sweet Silence studios since September, and most of the hard work was finished. Swedish producer Flemming Rasmussen, who had also worked on *Ride the Lightning*, was running the sessions, and various studio dudes milled about: roadies, engineers, friends of friends. It was hard to tell who was actually in the band; they all looked and acted alike. There were no stars in the room in those days—just soldiers.

The group was staying at the SAS Hotel in Copenhagen; Hammett and Burton shared one room, while Ulrich and Hetfield—Metallica's guiding forces—bunked together in another. "We thought we were just on top of the world!" Hammett recalls today. "We had almost all the songs written long before we got there. The only two songs that weren't finished were 'Orion' and 'The Thing That Should Not Be.' " Hammett still has preproduction tapes that the band "recorded on a boom box in the middle of the room" in El Cerrito. "We were having so much fun together that the songs kinda wrote themselves."

If the recording process itself had been difficult, it wasn't evident during my visit. A playback of the as-yet unmixed title track sounded astonishingly good, which might be expected of most things cranked out at ear-splitting volume in a professional recording studio. But when they played the recordings of "Battery" and the recently completed "Orion," it became evident that there was more to Metallica than skateboards and skull rings. Suddenly, they sounded like a band that a major label might sign to a multimillion-dollar contract.

Later that night, as we settled in for our interview at a downtown Copenhagen restaurant, I hoped to learn more about the group's apparent change of fortune; Lars, however, made it clear that he had an agenda of his own. He seemed keen to play down the fact that Elektra had obviously put some real money into the band, claiming that favorable exchange rate had allowed the band to spend months working on the album. As for the foreign recording location, Copenhagen was chosen, he said, because Rasmussen liked it, though one suspected the Danish-born Ulrich did, too. It later transpired that the others had found the bitterly cold Danish winter, with its short, dark days, tough to bear. Burton had difficulty staying focused once his bass parts were laid down and briefly returned home to San Francisco.

Listening to Ulrich, it was obvious that the group wanted finally to be taken seriously. "We've always had a serious attitude toward what we do," he said at one point, "especially in the studio. On our days off we might have a couple of these"—he indicated the Elephant beer—"but working on an album, you need to keep a clear head." It was quite a change from the drunken goofball personas they had exhibited just a couple of years before.

And while sales were obviously important to them, their main hope was to earn the respect of fans and critics. Clearly, they were still trying to determine how to maintain their integrity while reaching for the brass ring—to keep to their roots while broadening their sound and, hopefully, appeal. Said Ulrich, "There has got to be a way to make it without sucking."

> "It wasn't until we started with Bob Rock that we really learned how to **nail a riff down like AC/DC or the Stones."**
> —*ULRICH*

At this point, Burton leaned in. "This is the closest we've come yet to doing something really cool," he said. "You can really hear the progression from the last album."

That was true. Yet it was baffling how so many of their more towering numbers went from fast to slow, usually just as the riff kicked in. The song that would become "Master of Puppets" was such a track: in their heyday, Sabbath would have killed for such a riff. Then, just as the song starts to take off, everything slows down. It seemed counter intuitive, if not downright self-defeating. Ulrich pondered this point, then replied: "I don't know that I've ever thought about that. I guess that's just the way we kinda like it." Years later, producer Bob Rock raised the same point with Ulrich and Hetfield when he first listened to the demos for what became the Black Album.

"I used to think it was cool, a sign of our fuck-you attitude to being commercial," Ulrich says today. "Now I realize it was just basically because we couldn't play. It wasn't until we started with Bob Rock that we really learned how to nail a riff down like AC/DC or the Stones. It's actually a lot harder to do but you don't know that until you finally try it."

As our Copenhagen dining experience wound down, questions remained: How would the thrash crowd respond to the new album? How did Metallica hope to reach a larger audience with the new album without releasing a single, a matter they had not yet discussed with the folks at Elektra, or anyone else apparently. Their answers would have to wait. In time, they would be revealed.

Master of Puppets was duly released in the U.S. on March 3, 1986. Though Elektra clearly had high hopes for its commercial success, having granted the band both the money and time required to do the job right, it still wasn't clear how the payoff could be achieved. At the time of the record's release, Bon Jovi's *Slippery When Wet* was the most popular rock album, its suggestive title serving up an inadvertent reference to the slick production qualities embraced by Bon Jovi and every other mainstream act of the day. Even Judas Priest and Iron Maiden had begun using synthesizers and sequencing technology on their albums *Turbo* and *Somewhere in Time*, respectively.

True, *Master of Puppets* benefited from an impressive post-production mix by veteran L.A. studio fixer Michael Wagener. Yet Metallica's refusal to release a single—let alone shoot a video—seemed as masochistic as their groove-killing tempo changes. Sure enough, despite generally positive reviews, the album sat low on the charts upon its release.

Musically, Metallica had achieved one of the goals they stated in Copenhagen: to stay true to their thrash roots while expanding their musical palette. "We wanted to make an album that left all that scene behind," Ulrich said years later, "something we took our time on and gave our best shot. Not something with a label." Yet, *Master of Puppets* had a lot in common with its predecessor, right down to the sequencing. Like *Ride the Lightning*, it began with a slow, atmospheric acoustic guitar intro before segueing into fast electric rock ("Battery," an oblique tribute to their old stomping ground, the Old Waldorf Club on San Francisco's Battery Street). This was followed by the epic title track and, four songs in, the token "ballad," "Welcome Home (Sanitarium)."

Peel back the album's outer skin, however, and it was clear there was more going on than just improving upon a successful template. The main difference was a huge leap forward in the quality of the songwriting. It's no coincidence that *Master of Puppets* was the first Metallica album to feature all-new material since the group's early days, when a pre-Megadeth Dave Mustaine, not Kirk Hammett, played alongside Hetfield. Gone were tunes about how hard they were gonna kick your ass. In their place were songs about more complicated subjects. According to Hetfield, the title track itself "deals pretty much with drugs, how things get switched around. Instead of you controlling what you're taking and doing, it's drugs controlling you." A closer reading of the song, though, coupled with the unequivocal imagery of the album sleeve—an apocalyptic field of white crosses manipulated by the strings of an unseen puppet master—seems to suggest a more metaphorical attack on the invisible forces of control that govern all our lives. As Hammett now says, the "concept" behind the whole album was one of "manipulation in all its various forms."

"The Thing That Should Not Be," which followed "Master of Puppets," was clearly inspired by the gothic horror tales of H.P. Lovecraft. Slow and evocative, it was the first of several songs on the album to escape the confines of thrash and shoot for something more original. Even so, the song's lyrical couplet "Not dead which eternal lie/Stranger eons death may lie" is a paraphrased quote from Lovecraft that had also graced the cover of Iron Maiden's live double album, *Live After Death*, which had been released while Metallica were in Copenhagen. It's hard to imagine that Lars, the quintessential Maiden fan in those days, hadn't been aware of it.

"Welcome Home (Sanitarium)," meanwhile, was another mid-paced attempt to break free of thrash. Written from the viewpoint of an unjustly incarcerated patient at a mental hospital—and destined, like the title track, to become a major highlight of Metallica's live shows over the next 10 years—the song plays upon themes of loneliness and social separation, subjects that would resurface in a more successful format on "One," a track to appear on their next album, ... *And Justice for All*. The next song, "Disposable Heroes," was a musically straightforward antiwar song that, as Ulrich said, "rocked like a bitch." Hammett recalls that the little guitar passage at the end of the verse was his attempt at a military march. "I watched a lot of war movies, trying to find something that was like a call to arms—like something the bagpipes would play as they were going into battle—[*and*] that's what I came up with."

Its follow-up, "Leper Messiah," is obviously about the hypocrisy of the TV evangelists that had become such an American phenomenon in the early Eighties. The title, taken from the lyric to David Bowie's 1972 track "Ziggy Stardust," also served as James and Lars' putdown of the Los Angeles production-line glam metal scene they had rejected in the band's earliest days, as exemplified by the line: "Join the endless chain/ Taken by his glamour..." Interestingly, Dave Mustaine later claimed to have co-written "Leper Messiah," though Hammett denies this.

"There's maybe a chord progression that was in that song—like maybe 10 seconds that came from him—that, ironically, is just before the guitar solo. But he did not write 'Leper Messiah' at all. In fact, I remember being in the room when Lars came up with the main musical motif."

More intriguingly, one of the major highlights of the album contained no lyrics at all, its message relying totally on the eloquence of Burton's soaring, hypnotic bass. Clocking in at eight minutes, "Orion" illustrates, perhaps better than any other track on the album, how far Metallica had come since the days of *Kill 'Em All*. Hammett recalls how the haunting bass part in the middle section (a gorgeous riff later sampled by DJ Shadow on his 1997 album, *Endtroducing...*) had "already been written by Cliff—with bass lines, two- and three-part harmonies, all completely arranged—while we were in El Cerrito. We were really blown away."

Ironically, "Damage, Inc.," the final track on the album that firmly bade farewell to Metallica's thrash origins, is the biggest thrash-out on the entire collection—an epic, in-your-face, bones-into-dust heavy metal behemoth. "I remember Cliff playing the intro to 'Damage, Inc.' on the *Ride the Lightning* tour," says Hammett. "It had all these bass swells and harmonies on it. Hammett recalls Burton telling him the piece is based on the J.S. Bach chorale prelude "Come Sweet Death."

Hetfield, meanwhile, used the finale to spell out the band's credo in the lines: 'Following our instinct not a trend/Go against the grain until the end.' More than anything else, *Master of Puppets* was the indisputable proof of that. Burton called it "the best thing we've ever done, period. You read bands saying that shit in magazines and it looks so fake, but that's how I feel about *Master*... We never got that far with something before."

He was right. Now firmly recognized as one of their two finest works—along with the Black Album—*Master of Puppets* is still the album you pull out to prove that this monumental, zillion-dollar, corporate monster we now know Metallica as does actually have a soul.

The refinements demonstrated on *Master of Puppets* showed Metallica as a group that had escaped the thrash ghetto and was now ready for anything. This was no longer "Metal Up Your Ass," as they had wanted to call their first album, but rock with its head out on the creative ledge—a phenomenon, with very few exceptions, not seen in the U.S. charts since the heyday of the Seventies.

"The cohesiveness from one track to the next made perfect sense to us," says Hammett. "It was almost as if the album created itself. From the beginning, when we started writing the songs, all the way to the end, really great ideas were just moving and coming out of nowhere in a nonstop flow. It was almost magical, because it seemed like everything we played went right, every note we played was in exactly the right spot, and it couldn't ever have gone any better. It was just a very, very special time."

Holding the album in his hands for the first time, Hammett says, he knew Metallica had created something unique and lasting. "I remember thinking, Wow, this is a fucking great album! Even if it doesn't sell anything, it doesn't matter to me because this is such a great musical statement that we've just created."

Having convinced everyone against releasing a single—"the songs were too long and they wouldn't get radio play anyway," says Hammett—Metallica hit the road to support *Master of Puppets* the only way they knew how. "We decided to just go on the road and tour until we dropped," says Hammett. "Which is literally what we did."

Despite the album's low chart performance, Metallica were signed up to open Ozzy Osbourne's U.S. tour, which began on March 27, 1986, at the Kansas Coliseum in Wichita. Black Sabbath fans to a man, Metallica were thrilled by the opportunity to tour with Osbourne. Ozzy, for his part, soon became convinced the group was mocking him. "All I used to hear coming out of their trailer backstage was old fucking Sabbath albums!" he recalls. But as Ulrich says, "You gotta remember, we're old Black Sabbath fans. Without Sabbath there would have been no Metallica. We were definitely in awe when we started out on that tour. Ozzy was a fucking legend to us. But by the end of it we'd had some good times with him."

By comparison, bands like Iron Maiden and Judas Priest, previously the epitome of hardcore metal, **now sounded positively middle-of-the-road.**

Of the band's nine-song set list, four were from the new album: "Battery," which opened the set; "Master of Puppets"; "Welcome Home (Sanitarium)"; and "Damage, Inc.," which closed the set. Between dates with Osbourne, Metallica played headlining shows at small venues. Thanks to their drive, *Master of Puppets* began to climb the charts, hitting Number 29 on the *Billboard* Hot 100 despite a complete lack of TV or radio exposure. The album reached Number 41 in the U.K. charts and did well in other countries as well. For the first time, Metallica had shown up on the international radar. Suddenly, whether you'd heard the album or not, you were obliged to have an opinion on it.

Or on the group itself. A *Newsweek* reporter on the tour described Metallica as "ugly," "smelly" and "obnoxious." He added: "I hate them. But you can't deny their success." In fact, the Ozzy/Metallica U.S. tour was the second-biggest ticket-selling draw on the American circuit that summer (only the Aerosmith/Ted Nugent tour out-grossed them). Sales of Metallica T-shirts also rocketed: a sure sign of success. By the time the U.S. tour ended at the Coliseum in Hampton, Virginia, on August 3, *Master of Puppets* had sold more than 500,000 copies in the U.S. alone, giving the band its first Gold record.

Master of Puppets brought Metallica to the mainstream, and the mainstream would never be the same. By comparison, bands like Iron Maiden and Judas Priest, previously the epitome of hardcore metal, now sounded positively middle-of-the-road. The sense of frustration and anger that permeates *Master of Puppets* resonated with a new generation of fans who didn't want their rock rouged or radio-friendly but hard-edged and uncompromising.

Hammett says he was stunned when *Master of Puppets* went Gold. "Until then, I thought people just didn't understand us. Maybe we're doing something that's going over people's heads. But as we went on that Ozzy tour, we converted a lot of people night after night. And it gave us a lot of hope just to carry on. Suddenly we were selling albums, and a lot of it had to do with just going out there and playing our asses off, putting on a great show, just bringing the music to the people in that way, because radio just wasn't having us."

He recalls having a meeting on the back of the tour bus with the band's manager, Cliff Bernstein. "He said, 'You guys will be able to put down-payments on houses. I'm just really proud of you.' And the first thing that Cliff said was, 'I want a house where I can shoot my gun that shoots knives!' That was such a typical Cliff Burton thing to say."

Perhaps no one embodied the true spirit of Metallica better than Cliff Burton. Although the songwriting chores had always been mainly the preserve of Hetfield and Ulrich, Burton was arguably the group's spiritual figurehead. Hetfield's image had yet to fully develop, while Ulrich's position as the group's de facto spokesman was reserved strictly for offstage pronouncements. Burton, on the other hand, had always cast the longest shadow in Metallica, both onstage and off.

Cruelly, *Master of Puppets*—the record that, as Burton said, had been such an achievement for the group—would be his swan song, and its tour his final journey.

In early August, Metallica completed its U.S. tour with Osbourne and enjoyed a five-week break. On September 10, the European leg of the tour got underway in the U.K. Following a celebratory appearance at London's prestigious Hammersmith Odeon theatre on September 21, Metallica headed for Sweden and, three days later, commenced touring in Lund. On September 26, Metallica appeared at the Solnahallen in Stockholm. The show ended with Burton pummeling out the riffs to "Damage, Inc." and "Blitzkrieg," his right arm windmilling wildly. It had been a good night. Hetfield had been able to play guitar again for the first time since he'd broken his wrist, and Burton had pulled off a show-stopping bass solo during an improvised and hugely emotional rendering of "The Star Spangled Banner." The mood was high on the tour bus later that night as they hurtled down the motorway to Copenhagen, the very city where the album had been born.

Earlier that night, the band had drawn cards to decide who got which bunk. Burton drew the ace of spades and got the bunk normally used by Hammett. At just past five o'clock that morning, the driver lost control of the bus, which skidded horrifyingly before rolling over into a roadside ditch. Burton was thrown through the glass window nearest his bunk, where he was sleeping, and crushed as the bus collapsed on top of him. A crane was brought to the scene to raise the vehicle, but it was already too late. Cliff Burton was just 24.

Ulrich broke a toe, Hammett and Hetfield were badly bruised, and then–tour manager Bobby Schneider dislocated his shoulder. Burton was the sole fatality. The bus driver was subsequently arrested by

Danish police and charged with manslaughter. (He would escape imprisonment and was even rumored to be driving bands around Europe again some years later.)

Anthrax, who had been the opening act on the tour, had received the news when they arrived in Copenhagen. The next day, Anthrax guitarist Scott Ian summed up the feelings of many: "From the first day that I met him to the last one we spent together in Stockholm, Cliff Burton never changed. Even with Metallica's growing success, he remained the same really nice guy I first got to know and like. His mode of dress and his manner never altered, and we're all gonna miss him terribly."

For many fans, the loss of Cliff represented the loss of the band's identity; even, perhaps, its soul.

Burton's funeral was held 10 days later in his northern California hometown of Castro Valley. His band mates were still in shock. "Orion" was played at the tearful service, which the band attended along with his friends and devastated family. Cliff's ashes were later spread over Maxwell Ranch, one of his favorite places.

There was some talk, initially, that Burton's death would also mean the end of Metallica. Instead, as we now know, the band's post-Burton career was the most unexpected success story. As Kirk said at the time, "It wouldn't be fair to Cliff to just stop. He would've wanted us to go on." That said, it is doubtful Metallica would have become as successful as they did had Burton not died. For one thing, it's impossible to imagine Cliff Burton agreeing to work with Bon Jovi producer Bob Rock, as they did four years later on the Black Album, the record that made them superstars.

For another, it's entirely plausible that Burton's death spurred Metallica to work harder and reach higher, to hold onto success even as events conspired to take it from them. Six weeks after his death, Metallica played their first show with Burton's replacement, former Flotsam and Jetsam bassist Jason Newsted, at the Country Club in Reseda, California. The world tour for *Master of Puppets* resumed, followed by the release of multi-Platinum albums like *...And Justice for All* in 1988 and, even more successfully, the Black Album in 1991. By then, it was hard to remember that Metallica had once been a weedy band of thrash-loving headbangers.

Yet for many fans, Burton's death represented the loss of the band's identity, even, perhaps, its soul. Indeed, 20 years on, he still casts such a shadow over the story of Metallica and, specifically, *Master of Puppets*. It has become, above all, Cliff's album, imbued with his uniquely individual personality, unshakable character, sheer courage, wry humor and deeply held musical beliefs.

"When Cliff left us, it was a huge loss," says Hammett, "in terms of losing a friend but also in terms of losing a very, very strong musical ally. I mean, he was a large influence on us not just as a bass player but also as a musician. He taught me about counterpoint. Cliff was the master of that—it came from his classical influence. He also had a really good melodic feel."

Hammett says that, for a bass player, Burton played a lot of guitar. "In fact, he would drive me crazy with it. We'd come back to the hotel after a night of gallivanting, like totally wasted at three in the morning. But instead of crashing out he would immediately want to set up the electric guitars and start playing for a couple of hours. I'd be exhausted, but then I'd totally get sucked into it and start playing along with him. He would talk me into figuring out the guitar parts of certain songs.

He was obsessed with Ed King, one of the guitar players in Lynyrd Skynyrd. He said that Ed King was his favorite guitar player."

Hammett maintains that, had Metallica made another album with Burton, it would have been "extremely melodic." "Right before he died, he was listening to Creedence Clearwater Revival, the Eagles, the Velvet Underground, Kate Bush... He listened to a *lot* of Bach, and he turned us onto R.E.M. At the same time he was also listening to a lot of Mercyful Fate, a lot of Motörhead, a lot of Zeppelin and Hendrix and Pink Floyd. Plus, he was really into Anthrax. So he really could have gone anywhere with his music."

Despite Burton's free-ranging musical tastes, Black Sabbath remained his favorite band and Geezer Butler his favorite bassist. "Geezer Butler's right-hand technique involved just hitting the strings with your fingers. Cliff called it 'floppy-finger technique' and said he had it too." As Hammett explains, a severed tendon prevented Burton from bending his right-hand pinkie. "It had no dexterity whatsoever, so he would just use it to hammer the strings and do anything to get a sound out of his bass."

Of course, Burton's influence extended beyond the stage. Says Hammett, "He was the most mature out of all of us. He had a quiet strength, was very, very confident, and the rest of us would defer to him in times of trouble. He just seemed so much wiser and much more responsible than the rest of us. He was the guy who would reprimand us and say, 'What the hell were you thinking?' or 'That was a really stupid thing to do!'

Burton, Hammett says, had "a lot of integrity," something he expressed in a stock sentence Hammett uses to this day: "It was, 'I don't give a fuck!' He was just very, very real. I don't know if he knew somehow that his time was limited but he really lived it like it was his last day, because he just wouldn't settle for anything other than what he believed in. And that taught me a lot. To this day there are things, situations that I'm going through and I can just picture Cliff saying, 'What's real to you? What's real to us in this situation? What really matters?' And he would go through a bunch of points that didn't really matter, naming them off, and at the end of each one he'd say: 'I don't give a fuck!' He was just a very, very strong guy, stubborn at times, and because of that he and I would clash sometimes. But we really were just bros. He was just a big influence on us all."

As such, *Master of Puppets* was both a beginning and an ending. You may argue about what those two things are, but one thing is for certain: Metallica would never record another album like it.

"That's probably why it's still my favorite Metallica album," says Hammett. "It was just an amazing time for us. We were putting all the right notes in all the right places." There was no attempt to make an album that would stand the test of time, he says. "That wasn't on our radar at all. We just wanted to make the best possible album we could at the time. We really just set our sights to that and buckled down. And we always felt that if we did indeed give it all we had and it didn't pan out the way we wanted to, at least we could say we tried our best. And that was our attitude."

He says that he played the album a day or so beforehand in preparation for our interview. Afterward, he was struck by a thought: "If you released this today, it would be right up there with all the newest releases in terms of sound, quality, production, concept... It's still relevant. Even the things James was writing about back then are still relevant. And you get the feeling it will all still be relevant tomorrow."

[5]

"I didn't want to become
a Van Halen clone."
—*KIRK HAMMETT*

METAL MILITIA

Back in 1988, Metallica took America by storm on
the Monsters of Rock tour and with the monster album
...And Justice for All. For 25-year-old Kirk Hammett,
it was an occasion that marked the guitarist's first
of many *Guitar World* cover interviews.

BY JEFF SPURRIER

TO ANY METALLICA MANIAC, the chain of events that transpired during the band's set at the L.A. Coliseum Monsters of Rock show was about as predictable as the clichéd, ham-fisted riffs churned out by the other acts on the bill. During Metallica's third song, an estimated 15,000 fans breached the wire barricade set up around the floor of the arena. Under the blistering mid-afternoon sun, the metal militia battered down a fence and rushed the stage in a lemming-like onslaught that left the yellow-jacketed security guards running for cover. "Alcoholica" read one of the banners unfurled among the mass of bodies. "Drink 'Em All" read another, a pun on the band's debut album, *Kill 'Em All*, as well as the group's dipsomaniacal reputation.

Throughout Metallica's performance, objects rained in from the crowd: shoes, hats, plastic spritzer bottles, shirts. At one point, drummer Lars Ulrich leaned over his drum riser at the rear of the stage and caught with one hand a thong sandal headed his way. He held it up like a trophy, grinned devilishly and gave a thumbs-up sign before throwing it back.

As the band played on, the frenzy of the audience shifted into overdrive, and soon the plastic chairs used for seating on the arena floor were being passed overhead toward the stage. Pieces of the chairs came flying in with the shoes and hats until finally a whole chair was thrown, nearly hitting singer James Hetfield. At that moment, the P.A. system conveniently gave out and the band quickly retired to the backstage area while efforts were made to defuse the near-riot mood.

After the band left the stage, thousands streamed out of the stadium, many stopping to buy $18 Metallica T-shirts from the concession stands. And although it was still early—Dokken, the Scorpions and Van Halen were still to come—some of the fans didn't bother to stick around.

"Metallica is why I came," said one 20-year-old Long Beacher. "I don't even know if I'm going to go back in. They kicked ass! They don't have copped-out attitudes. Their music is so perfect, and they're not a bunch of assholes. They've mastered what they do. They're speed metal, but they have melodic things in there too, which you don't see from a lot of speed metal bands. Usually it's just straight-out thrash. There's nobody to compare Kirk Hammett to—except maybe Randy Rhoads."

If you had to pick someone to inherit the mantle of fallen metal legend Randy Rhoads, you couldn't find a more unlikely candidate than 25-year-old Kirk Hammett. But then, there's little about Metallica that fits neatly preconceived notions. Although Metallica are one of the leading proponents of speed metal, the band has distinguished itself from its peers with complex song structures, issue-oriented lyrics, long songs that defy handy radio formatting and an appreciation for melody even within the overamped environment of metal, a genre not known for subtlety. With their reliance upon word-of-mouth popularity and a casual, down-to-earth style, the band has become a true grassroots phenomenon. Considering the wild enthusiasm evident at the Monsters shows, critics are already predicting that the band's next album, ...*And Justice for All*, will hit Number One.

The key, says Hammett, is originality. "We've gotten as far as we have because we offer something different," he says. "There were bands like Motörhead and Diamond Head doing this before us; we were just at the right place at the right time. There are a lot of thrash metal bands that wouldn't even think of doing a ballad. We've had a ballad on every album since [*1984's*] *Ride the Lightning*. We're not afraid to try different things, like slowing down arrangements or not screaming all the time or singing real melodies. Even on the leads I play, I try to be as different as possible. Everyone now is trying to do this Yngwie Malmsteen thing—playing at 10 thousand miles an hour—and everyone does it better than I do, so I don't even bother."

In a hotel room the day after the L.A. Coliseum show, Hammett sits back on the sofa and props his legs up on a coffee table. With his hair pulled back, his glasses on and a whisper of a mustache, he looks much younger than his actual age. Somewhat shy and self-effacing, Hammett doesn't come across like one might expect one of speed metal's leading lights to. At the previous day's red-hot performance he performed arpeggios and three-octave scales with casual aplomb. In person, however, he seems guilelessly insecure, readily acknowledging his ongoing struggle to blend technical expertise with the band's herky-jerky tempos and convoluted song structure.

There's no posturing, no canned answers, no self-aggrandizement. In fact, one of the first things he says is that the spotlight on him should be broadened to include rhythm guitarist James Hetfield.

Hammett started playing guitar 10 years ago while a teenager in the small San Francisco Bay Area town of El Sobrante. Like fledgling players everywhere, he spent years trying to find the right combination of components that would give him the perfect sound. His first rig, "a piece-of-shit Montgomery Ward electric guitar and a cardboard shoe-box amp with a four-inch speaker," was abandoned after a few weeks. He borrowed a neighbor's Stella, played it for a few years and then got his first real guitar, a 1978 Strat.

"I could never get a full sound out of it," he recalls, "mostly because I was playing through shit amps. I did a lot of experimenting with it, putting in different pickups. I tried DiMarzios, Bill Lawrence humbuckers and some others. I never knew that full sound I heard on records was coming through beefed-up Marshalls. Later, I managed to get hold of a Randall bass amp, but I still wasn't successful. Then I got a Sunn amp with CMOS technology and solid-state distortion, and that was it—I finally had that overdriven, distorted sound. I traded in my Strat and for $200 more I got a '74 Gibson Flying V. I had just discovered Michael Schenker and thought he was great."

With his Flying V (which he still frequently uses on record) and Sunn amp, Hammett started playing in bands, only to face a new problem. The sound became too distorted. After a stint at Burger King, he earned enough money to buy a Marshall half-stack and finally found the right mix.

Metallica recruited him to join just before the band made its first album, 1983's *Kill 'Em All*. "I played my first gig with them a week later on the East Coast, and actually, they never told me I was in the band," he says with a laugh. "After we were in the studio making the album, I figured I was in."

Around the same time, Hammett met up with the person who would drastically alter his approach to the guitar: Berkeley guitar teacher Joe Satriani.

"In 1982 and 1983, the heavy metal scene in San Francisco was really healthy and fruitful. There were a lot of bands and a lot of competition between guitar players. I found out then that there were two types of [*metal*] guitar players: your basic Eddie Van Halen clone and your stylized heavy metal player. I didn't want to become a Van Halen clone. And there was this one guitar player [*on the club circuit*] whose style I really liked. He was doing arpeggios and three-octave solos, so I asked him where he learned his stuff. He told me about Joe, so I called him and started taking lessons from him. I took about 20 lessons over five years."

For the first time, Hammett was learning how and why certain metal guitarists chose certain scales and riffs. Satriani explained why some licks worked and why others didn't. "Eventually," Hammett recalls, "I stopped bringing him stuff to show me and we just concentrated on theory. We studied chord chemistry, modes, how to build scales off of different degrees and chord progressions. [*The results of the lessons*] became really apparent in 1984 and 1985. That was when my whole style really changed. He showed me how to harmonize with the band. And I've been applying what I learned from Joe over the last four years. After a while, the band couldn't tell what was influenced by Joe and what wasn't."

Satriani isn't the only guitarist Hammett cites as inspirational; Jimi Hendrix, Ulrich Roth and Michael Schenker all are on his list of influences. In fact, he says, he admires just about anybody who plays "a really good guitar solo."

And what's that?

"Something that's melodic, intense, aggressive and has hooks in it," he says. "Someone like George Lynch has a really bluesy feel in the middle of all these pyrotechnics. He'll do these wild hammer-ons and sweep arpeggios and then go into something really melodic that harmonizes. Gary Moore can also be really melodic and intense at the same time. And Steve Vai—he has a huge sense of humor in his playing, like he's cracking jokes with his guitar. And Joe—he has a lot of melody and he's really catchy and dynamic. That's so important. It's like the old saying of trying to tell a story with your guitar. It's a cliché, but it's true."

Even after his years of study with Satriani, Hammett admits that he's still not totally confident with his technique. When he's off the road, he plays constantly—immediately after waking up, during the afternoon, watching TV at night—and captures anything he likes on a Fostex four-track recorder.

Hammett always begins these workouts with exercises. "Scales, arpeggios, chromatic exercises—although I have trouble memorizing scales," he admits. "Especially three-octave modes. They're the hardest to memorize when you play them in cycles of fourths. Before we go onstage, I'll go through my modes in cycles of fourths and jam on parts of songs, trying to come up with something new. I practice scales every day, at least until I feel warmed up."

No amount of warming up eased the pressure the band felt going in to record their latest release. During the ...And Justice for All sessions, Metallica were getting ready for the Monsters of Rock tour, and rather than enjoying his usual relaxed schedule to polish his solos, Hammett found himself working long hours trying to make things work.

"From a technical point of view, this album was a nightmare," he grimaces. "There were so many tempo changes. James would come up with a rhythm background, and the only scale that would fit would be a minor pentatonic scale with a flatted fifth. Trying to be melodic in an altered scale like that was a nightmare. In 'Blackened,' there are four different tempo and rhythm background changes, and for me to make it smooth all the way through was really challenging. To this day, I don't think I did it successfully. People tell me differently, but in my head I know otherwise.

"There's something about being in the studio, in the heat of the moment when the red light goes on, that just makes you want to change things around," he continues. "After playing to rehearsal tapes for three months where it's slightly out of tempo and the recording isn't the best, suddenly you're in there hearing perfect drum tracks, perfect guitar tracks—everything is picture perfect. It really bothers me. I did all my leads for the album in seven days because I had to. The Monsters tour was coming up. When you do stuff that quickly, you settle for something, and when you go back and listen to it you may discover it's not happening. Things sound forced. I was working 16 hours a day doing solos, and when you work that long you start to lose your perspective. Your ear goes down the drain."

There was one aspect to the *Justice* recording that was not a nightmare for Hammett: getting the tone he wanted from his guitar. Unlike the *Master of Puppets* sessions, when he spent three days in the studio trying to get the right sound, this time the tone came a little easier.

"I knew what I wanted," he says. "During *Master*, I wasn't 100 percent sure. There's nothing more discouraging than working on something for eight hours and at the end of the session knowing it's crap. I think the guitar tones on this album are some of the better lead tones I've gotten. The rhythm sound that James got is amazing. We didn't have time to do anything super weird, which I wanted to do. I wanted to experiment a lot more."

The *Justice* recording contrasts sharply with *The $5.98 E.P.: Garage Days Re-Revisited*, the band's 1987 five-song compilation of British heavy metal and punk covers. The EP was released following a pair of nearly devastating incidents: the death of original bassist Cliff Burton in a bus accident in Sweden and a skateboarding injury that left Hetfield with a broken arm. The imposed hiatus found the band members getting back to their roots in a converted garage in Oakland, jamming on old Misfits and Diamond Head songs. The EP was recorded in six days with little concern for mistakes, bad notes or feedback. It's certainly not one of the best-recorded metal albums, but it is immediately seductive for its charm and youthful naiveté. It feels like an extension of one of Metallica's off-time country jams, when they get together with their friends in the Bay Area, retreat to a ranch outside the city and play wild garage tribal thrash long into the night.

Comparing *Garage Days* to *...And Justice for All* is like watching a time-lapsed film of a plant emerging from a seed. There's maturity, sophistication and a sense of direction present in songs like "Blackened," "One" and "Dyers Eve" that should propel Metallica out of cult status into mainstream popularity. Despite speed metal's teenage aura, Metallica are clearly not just for the angst-and-acne set. The attitude that emerges from their lyrics, personal style and musical technique shows that this is a band that refuses to play down—either to themselves or their audience.

"I'm not into that whole Satanic thing," Hammett says, obviously embarrassed by the symbolism some metal bands employ. "It's something to fall back on if you don't have much imagination. Singing your 50th song about having lunch with Satan—I'm not into it. It's silly. I see people out there trying to be so macho and heavy and I think, You've got to be kidding. You can't actually try to push this on an audience and expect them to believe it. But people get away with it. I feel if you can't take the band seriously, then you can't take the music seriously. For a group like that to sing about the crisis in Central America...come on, it would never work."

On the other hand, Metallica's lyrics, which are penned by Hetfield, do work. Containing themes of nuclear destruction, censorship and McCarthy-era "witch hunts," they are frequently bleak and stark, but it's not just for shock value. The band insists on having a lyric sheet on the inner sleeve of its albums so that its audience gets the message. "With heavy music you should have heavy lyrics," Hammett says. "Not just, 'Hey baby, let's drink a lot and puke on each other all night!' "

A good example is "One," from ...And Justice for All, which was inspired by Dalton Trumbo's classic antiwar story, Johnny Got His Gun. " 'One' is one of my favorite songs on that album," Hammett says. "I thought we captured the entire mood and the chain of events told in the book." The song "The Shortest Straw" is about the anti-Communist investigations led by U.S. senator Joseph McCarthy in the Fifties, which led to the blacklisting of many writers and entertainers. "Something like [McCarthyism] almost happened with the PMRC," Hammett says, referring to the Parents Music Resource Center co-founded by Tipper Gore in 1985, which pushed the music industry to use parental-warning labels on products that contain explicit lyrics. "If Tipper Gore's husband [Al Gore] hadn't been running for president, I think it would have gotten a lot worse. They had a picture of us in her book and the caption was, 'This band promotes alcohol.' It was pretty funny, actually."

As Hammett speaks, MTV flickers from a silent TV nearby, and he stares blankly at the sight of a popular glam band prancing around the stage, all flash and makeup. "For a band that doesn't play very well, they sure do have a lot of guitars," he mutters.

Like his band mates, Kirk Hammett doesn't believe in setting himself up on a pedestal, removed from the fans. Their following has been built by word of mouth, not hype or MTV or radio play. There was some discussion before *Justice* was completed about recording shorter songs—the shortest song on *Master of Puppets* is over five minutes, while others are over eight minutes long—but the ultimate decision was to go with what they like. Demographically, Hammett says, "People who listen to the radio probably aren't our type of crowd."

Similarly, jumping on bandwagons or following trends is simply not the Metallica way. After some persistent probing, Hammett admits that he does have some classical influences, but he doesn't like talking about them.

"Everyone says, 'Oh, I'm a heavy metal guitarist, but I'm classically influenced,' " he groans. "It's so trendy that I hate to talk about it. But one of my favorite all-time albums is *Christopher Parkening Plays Bach*. I love that. I went to see him with some friends seven months ago, and he was brilliant."

But is Kirk Hammett as brilliant in his chosen field? It's hard to say just yet. There's no doubt that the technical prowess is there; but as he himself concludes, that's not all there is to it.

"It's weird," he says, somewhat wearily. "I've found that, with all this study of technique, when you get right down to it, you throw all that out the window and go with what works best. I believe you have to have technique, but it's also good to detach yourself from all of it and go with what feels good. Just because you know umpteen billion scales, it doesn't mean you have to use them all in a solo."

It's just such an awareness that filters out the technicians from the artists, and Kirk Hammett seems to have the humility and love of his instrument to propel him into genuine superstardom. He's only 25, so who knows?

[**6**]

"Seven months in the studio
with Metallica
tends to change a man."
—*JAMES HETFIELD*

BLACK REIGN

Just weeks from completing Metallica's
breakthrough hit, the Black Album, James Hetfield
and Kirk Hammett invited *Guitar World* into
the studio for a revealing talk about their
metal masterpiece.

BY JEFF GILBERT

S JAMES HETFIELD NOTES in the following interview, the United States launched and completed the first Gulf War in less time than it took Metallica to finish their 1991 multi-Platinum breakthrough release. Titled simply *Metallica*, but more commonly known as the Black Album, the record brought Metallica into the mainstream and launched a new era for metal. In the months before its completion, *Guitar World* paid a studio visit to guitarists James Hetfield and Kirk Hammett as they put the finishing touches on the album. While our heroes were tired after months of hard work, they were clearly pleased with the results of their efforts.

"We've been in the studio so long, a war has come and gone, and we're still stuck in here!" A heavy weariness, quite evident behind James Hetfield's steely gaze, underscores the intense pressure that has been Metallica's constant companion over the past few months as they've labored to record *Metallica*, their first album in more than three years, and fifth overall. "It's pretty amazing when you think about it," Hetfield offers with a strained smile.

Here within the comfortable confines of One on One Studios in North Hollywood, it's down to the 11th hour for the world's greatest metal band. Working exhaustively around the clock with producer Bob Rock, Hetfield and Kirk Hammett take turns spit-polishing a guitar solo here and roughing out a vocal there. While this modern recording facility is outfitted with pool tables, weights, a well-stocked kitchen, dartboards, big-screen TVs, exercise machines and just about any creature-comfort a healthy (or otherwise) rock group could ever want, it has been a veritable Devil's Island for Metallica.

"We've been in the studio so long, **a war has come and gone,** and we're still stuck in here!"
—*HETFIELD*

"We've seen four other bands come through and do their albums," Hetfield notes. "And some of those guys have already gone on tour!"

Outside, a small group of roving Metallica fans, hoping to catch a glimpse of James or Kirk entering (but never, it seems, leaving) the white, windowless stucco building, maintains a tireless vigil, shuffling up and down the 5200 block of Lankershim Boulevard. Their nervous, darting eyes and untucked Metallica shirts have some local business proprietors double-checking their wares and wallets.

"This has been going on since last October, once them kids found out this heavy metal band was next door," says a leathery-looking taco vendor a block away. "They don't scare me none, though." As if on cue, a few scruffy fans wander in and order some burritos.

Inside the studio, Bob Rock is screaming. His voice penetrates the bank-vault thickness of the studio doors, almost reaching the street outside. The producer is at the hair-pulling stage after spending the past five-and-a-half hours trying to correct a single, renegade guitar note that, to his million-dollar ears, is a microscopic tone out of whack. "He's not having a good day," Hammett suggests with a sheepish grin. The guitarist is repeatedly called in to try to punch in a note that will allow the visibly stressed Canadian producer to finally wrap up the tedious session. Kirk excuses himself, runs into the studio's main room, shoulders a black ESP and effortlessly runs through the solo for the 20th time. "I think I got it," he says.

It's no small wonder that Bob Rock—the career-rescuing hit-maker for artists like Mötley Crüe, Aerosmith, the Cult and Bon Jovi—is concerned with something as seemingly trivial as a single guitar note. Taking on the Metallica project was a critical step in his otherwise Top 40–oriented career. "People will be saying Bob made Metallica sound like Bon Jovi," James remarks. "They don't realize that no one screws with us, except us. Bob fit right into the program and the direction we were going."

Certainly, Rock's commercially successful background has raised more than a few eyebrows among Metallica's many supporters. The notion of Hetfield and company opting for the producer's trademark approach—crisp, clear guitars and radio-friendly hooks—is enough to severely traumatize fans who drink in sledgehammer chords like their mother's milk.

"We're not really out to justify what we're doing," Hetfield says defensively. "We don't give a shit. This is what we want and this is how it is. Bob just helped us get what we want."

What they wanted for *Metallica*, and what they got, were guitars that ring more sharply than ever, leaving a clean trail of resonating destruction. Where ...*And Justice for All* was weak and flat-sounding in the bass and drum mix, the new album bursts with a deep snare crack and a bass thick and heavy enough to set cement with. The band's whiplash tempo changes and complicated arrangements have been revamped into a lethal and immensely heavy, groove-laden sound and album that should give thrash a sharp kick in its sluggish ass.

"Kirk!" Rock's screams are getting louder.

"Uh-oh," Hammett says, jumping up like a dog about to be punished for knocking over the garbage can. "Got to go."

GUITAR WORLD Your patented "Metalli-crunch" seems bigger and badder than ever on the new album. What did you do to fatten your sound?

KIRK HAMMETT First, I went through my CD collection and picked out guitar sounds that impressed me and gave them to Bob as points of reference. It helps to know what kind of tone you're trying to pursue.

GW What discs did you give him?

HAMMETT I was particularly impressed with Gary Moore's sound on his latest album, *Still Got the Blues*. I used one of the breaks from "Oh, Pretty Woman" as a main reference. I also gave him UFO's *Obsession*—I've always liked Michael Schenker's sound. The third example was something by Carlos Santana. I was shooting for a real upfront sounding guitar.

GW But wasn't that the problem with ...*And Justice for All*? The guitar was so upfront that it obscured Jason's [*Newsted*] bass.

JAMES HETFIELD The bass was obscured for two reasons. First, on [*the* Garage Days Re-Revisited *EP*], Jason tended to double my rhythm guitar parts, so it was hard to tell where my guitar started and his bass left off. Also, my tone on *Justice* was very scooped—all lows and highs with very little midrange. When my rhythm parts were placed in the mix, my guitar sound ate up all the lower frequencies. Jason and I were always battling for the same space in the mix.

On this album, Jason approached his parts differently. He's playing more with Lars' kick drum, so his bass lines are very distinct from my guitar lines; we're not getting in each other's way. Bob really helped us with orchestrating and bringing out the low end—getting the guitar and bass to work together. In fact, when I played the album for a friend, he asked, "What is that weird low-end sound?" I said, "That's something new for us. It's called bass!"

GW Did Bob understand the Metallica guitar sound?

HETFIELD Oh yeah, and he actually added to it. After we recorded some of the new album, we pulled out the actual master tapes from *Justice* and singled out the guitar sound. I discovered something that I already knew—that my *Justice* sound lacked body. As I mentioned earlier, midrange has always been a no-no for me, but Bob showed me that having a touch of it in there really adds to your tone.

I think he was a little intimidated at the start because he wasn't sure how far he could push us. Bob was trying to be real professional, so we had to loosen him up. He was really polite at first and would say things like, "It's your album, do whatever you want" and "It's only my opinion, but how about if we try this?" [*laughs*] However, seven months in the studio with Metallica tends to change a man. And Bob's been changed. [*laughs*] He's got a few more gray hairs, a few more wrinkles. He grew a tumor and has some sore knuckles from hitting the studio walls.

HAMMETT Yeah, he really loosened up. In no time he was scream-ing and yelling and saying stuff like, "You have to get angry for this part. Play it really mean and dirty!" Then we'd record another part and he'd say, "Be bluesy and bendy." And to illustrate his point, Bob would move his shoulders all around. I'd just stare at him like he was a madman, thinking, Uh, well, okay. But his approach eventually worked. I really started focusing on what he was trying to say. He encouraged me to think conceptually, not with my fingers. I thought a lot about what I felt would be the best way to approach the solo from a mental standpoint. As a result, my solos turned out smoother and more confidently executed.

> "A lot of bands put out the same record three or four times, and **we didn't want to fall into that rut.**"
> —*HAMMETT*

GW Were you ever afraid that Bob was going to turn Metallica into a pop band?

HETFIELD Some people thought Bob would make us sound too commercial. You know: "Oh, Bob works with Bon Jovi, Bob works with Mötley Crüe." But if [*former Metallica producer*] Flemming Rasmussen worked on a Bon Jovi record, would Bon Jovi all of a sudden sound like Metallica? We chose Bob because we were really impressed with his crisp, full-sounding production on the Cult's *Electric* album and on Mötley Crüe's *Dr. Feelgood*.

HAMMETT We wanted to create a different record and offer something new to our audience. I hate it when bands stop taking chances. A lot of bands put out the same record three or four times, and we didn't want to fall into that rut.

The truth is, we may have been guilty in the past of putting out the same running order—you know, start out with a fast song, then the title track, then a ballad. Other than that, though, we've really tried to create something different every time we went into the studio. And on *Metallica*, we made a conscious effort to alter and expand the band's basic elements.

GW Did you experiment with different amps and cabinets?

HETFIELD We tried a bunch of amps, but I ended up using the same Mesa/Boogie Simul-class Mark II that I've used on the last three albums. In Los Angeles there are a million amps you can try out, but none of them were up to snuff. Bob also brought in a bunch of crappy-looking vintage amps. We gave everything a shot and ended up with the same old shit. [*laughs*]

I must admit, though, it was a lot of fun trying out all those little Sixties and Seventies amps—they really sounded unique. A lot of metal players have forgotten that they can be useful. We used a couple of vintage amps for texture. But I wasn't about to play a rhythm part through a fucking Fender Supro amp, you know? We sure as hell weren't making *Led Zeppelin I*.

GW Kirk, what did you use for amplification?

HAMMETT I used a Bradshaw preamp for the lows and mids, and a couple of Marshalls for the nice clean highs. We EQ'd it through the board a little bit, and it worked out great.

The miking process was pretty simple. Bob had an engineer move a mic around in front of the cabinet until I heard the sound I wanted.

GW Is your studio setup the same as your live setup?

HETFIELD My live sound doesn't work in the studio; it's a completely different animal. Every little thing is detrimental to the sound. And if someone moves a mic after we've got the sound we want, then it's lost. It's pretty much a case of "lock the door and set up a police line."

GW What do you look for in an amp?

HETFIELD A smooth, solid, round sound. Something that doesn't sound fake. You can always fiddle around with the EQ later. A lot of modern amps and preamps sound great when you're jamming by yourself, but they don't hold up in a band situation. The sound isn't dense enough, and the lows and highs tend to get soaked up by the bass and cymbals.

GW James, you also tried a variety of guitars, which seems a little out of character for you.

HETFIELD My primary guitar was an ESP Explorer with EMG pickups, but I also used a Telecaster, a Gretsch White Falcon with a Bigsby and a Guild 12-string. I used the other guitars just for bits and pieces.

GW Kirk, I understand you didn't use your '74 Gibson Flying V on this record. What was your primary ax?

HAMMETT I used two guitars: a Strat-style ESP with two EMGs and an '89 Gibson Les Paul Deluxe with two EMGs. The way I settled on those guitars is pretty funny. At the beginning of the recording process, I laid down one of my solos 15 times, using 15 different guitars. Then I listened to each track and, without knowing which guitar was which, selected the tone that sounded the best. I finally narrowed it down to the ESP and the Les Paul.

GW And you nailed the solo perfectly each time?

HAMMETT Well, not exactly. [*laughs*] Good enough to A-B them, though. It was kind of interesting to play all those different guitars. Bob brought in a lot of different guitars, too. He's a guitar player—or so he says. [*laughs*]

GW What happened to your black '74 Gibson Flying V?

HAMMETT I used that V on every album prior to this one, but the ESP just sounded a bit rounder. Also, I felt it was time for a change. I bought that V while working at a Burger King. I worked three months—just long enough to be able to afford it. As soon as I made $400, I quit. I don't even know how much it costs to buy a guitar these days. I haven't set foot in a guitar store in ages.

GW The songs on the new album are shorter than usual.

HETFIELD "Metallica" shorter. Six minutes instead of 10.

GW It should be easier to get some radio airplay.

HETFIELD That was always a problem. We'd record a song that people liked and wanted to hear on the radio, and the radio bastards wouldn't play it because it was too long. Or they would want to edit it, which we wouldn't allow.

But radio airplay wasn't the whole idea behind us writing shorter songs. It just seemed to us that we had pretty much done the longer song format to death. We were only able to fit about 12 songs in a two-and-a-half-hour show. These shorter songs are going to help a bit—we're going to be able to play more of 'em. [*laughs*] We have one song that has just two riffs in it, which is pretty amazing. It only takes two minutes to get the point across.

GW Shorter songs mean shorter guitar solos.

HAMMETT In some instances.

GW Also, the new album is less complex, harmonically.

HAMMETT That's true. There are fewer key changes. There aren't many flatted fourth progressions or anything like that—just straight-ahead major and minor keys. The most complex song is probably "Wherever I May Roam," which suggests a Phrygian dominant scale.

GW Metallica has acquired a reputation for being meticulous in the studio. How often do you go back and repair something you think could be improved?

HAMMETT I fix things all the time. Every time I do a solo, I recheck it and correct things that don't hit the mark.

GW In doing so, do you ever get the feeling that your behavior is less musical than it is...anal retentive?

HAMMETT [*laughs*] It's like this—you have to live with it. When you know you're going to be listening to a performance over 500 times, it's important to be happy with it. Believe me, there are mistakes on our other albums, and I can't bring myself to listen to them. It's torture.

GW Which cuts?

HAMMETT I'm not going to say! [*laughs*] You have to pick them out yourself.

GW What really stands out about *Metallica* is its feel.

HETFIELD That's what we wanted—a live feel. In the past, Lars and I constructed the rhythm parts without Kirk and Jason, or Lars played to a click by himself. This time I wanted to try playing as a band unit in the studio. It lightens things up, and you get more of a vibe. Everyone was in the same room, and we were able to watch each other. That helped a lot, especially with some of the bass and lead stuff. It also helped that we'd played most of the songs for two months before we entered the studio.

Unfortunately, Lars kind of pussied out at the end. He didn't want everyone there. I guess it's kind of difficult to work in the studio when you're not used to a new song and there are all these people around.

GW Lars is always very involved in the Metallica production process. What is his input with regard to the guitar sound?

HETFIELD He doesn't mess with the guitar sound—just the bass guitar. [*laughs*] He can say whatever he wants, but I think he's pretty confident in my ability to know what's right as far as the guitar goes.

GW While the songs on *Metallica* are less complex, the orchestration on this album is more sophisticated than on your previous efforts.

HETFIELD That's right. I think the degree of subtlety may shock people. Bob's really good with sound, and we took advantage of that by using different guitars and more vocal harmonies.

There are fewer guitar overdubs on this record, though. I used to layer 80 guitars in my attempt to create a heavy sound. While making this album, I discovered that sheer quantity doesn't necessarily make for a heavier sound; if anything, overdubs make guitars sound mushier. As far as rhythms go, there are either two or three tracks, and they're split pretty evenly. There is a lot more separation on this album, which also makes it sound punchier. With a pair of headphones, you can tell who's doing what.

GW Were there any songs that didn't make it to the album?

HETFIELD No. We went in and recorded 12. There are no other half-written songs sitting around anywhere. Whatever we wrote is there. It only takes one day of trying to write something to tell if it's going to end up in the dumper. [*laughs*]

GW Kirk, "The Unforgiven" features an unusual solo. How did it evolve?

HAMMETT That was probably the most challenging solo on the album. I had something worked out before I got into the studio, but Bob felt it wasn't quite appropriate. He asked if I could try something dirtier and more sustaining—something more in the Jeff Beck vein. At first I was kind of hurt, but then I realized he was right. I started fingerpicking a chordal thing, and Bob liked the way it sounded. He said, "Why don't you play that entire guitar solo with your fingers and really pull on the strings and slap them against the frets?" It was a cool idea. I did it, and it sounded really percussive. That was the first time I fingerpicked a guitar solo on an album.

GW Did you do anything that challenged your harmonic capabilities?

HAMMETT "Of Wolf and Man" reminded me of some of the more progressive music on *Justice*. The rhythm parts jumped from a I chord to a fV chord—from E to B♭—which always presents a problem. I was stumped at first, but after a while I just started singing various lines and adapting my vocal melodies for the guitar. I discovered that singing breaks down a lot of imaginary boundaries, and disrupts that tendency to gravitate toward familiar scales and finger patterns on the guitar.

GW Does the band offer much input regarding your guitar solos?

HAMMETT Sometimes I need an objective opinion, and it's good to ask the guys. But you know, I'll only change so much. [*laughs*] They'll make suggestions, but they never tell me what to play. It's more like, "I'm going to play what I think feels good, and if you don't like it, you tell me, and maybe I'll change it."

"I can't play leads. My strength is in writing riffs."
—*HETFIELD*

We had a really big argument about a certain guitar solo. I said, "No, this is the way I want it to turn out." And that's the way we kept it. But it's good to have an objective opinion around, because it can lead to other areas and directions you didn't consider in the first place.

GW For example?

HAMMETT The solo that really comes to mind is the one in "The God That Failed." I had this whole thing worked out, and Bob said, "I don't know if that's going to make it. Try something like this." And he half sang, half mumbled something. The only things really audible were the first three out of the eight or nine notes he was trying to sing. So I took those three notes and came up with a phrase that actually worked very well. Between his singing and my interpretation, we mapped out a solo that was a lot different from my original idea.

GW James, why is it that you don't play any solos?

HETFIELD I can't play leads. I can do really cool harmony shit, and on slow songs I can do bendy-feely-type shit, but my strength is in writing riffs. I just have a better feel for rhythm. I'll never be able to play fast like Kirk. I don't even try, because he's the man. He's using a lot of wah-wah lately, which everyone in the band really loves.

GW Kirk, your use of the wah-wah pedal has almost become your signature.

HAMMETT There's something about a wah pedal that really gets my gut going. People will probably say, "He's just hiding behind the wah," but that isn't the case. It's just that those frequencies really bring out a lot of aggression in my approach. Much of my playing is rhythmic and choppy; I use a lot of double stops. The wah just accents all those stops and chops and brings out the rhythmic aspect that much more.

The only problem I've had with my Vox wah is its tendency to move around on the floor. So now it sits on a rubber mat that says in big letters, "Kirk's Wah-Wah Rug." [*laughs*]

GW Your solos on this album seem much more fluid than those you played in the past. What's your secret?

HAMMETT We toured for a year and a half before we recorded this album, and that really helped my playing a lot. I also started listening to different kinds of music, which helped broaden my perspective. For example, I've been experimenting with slide guitar.

I also discovered a new recording process that really works for me. On *Metallica*, I recorded six or seven different guitar solos for almost every song, took the best aspects of each solo, mapped out a master solo and made a composite. Then I learned how to play the composite solo, tightened it up and replayed it for the final version. The only bad thing about that process is that it led to a lot of arguments.

GW Didn't being in the studio for so long drive you crazy?

HETFIELD Yes, it did! [*laughs*] Very much so. I don't remember doing anything else. I don't remember not living in the studio. I'm itching for people to hear this album because I'm sick of hearing it myself. That's the ultimate feeling—when someone hears your shit and says, "That's good!" And I go, "I know, but it's good to hear you say it!"

[7]

"I never had much of a
social life in high school,
and was always kind of shy and introverted."
—KIRK HAMMETT

BORN TO BURN

Kirk Hammett: Why I Play Guitar.

as told to *HAROLD STEINBLATT*

WHEN I WAS GROWING UP in San Francisco during the Seventies, I used to hang around with my brother and his college friends. When my family moved to a small suburb, he stayed in the city. I missed him a lot, and to fill the void, I listened to a lot of the same music he would listen to: Hendrix, Zeppelin, Cream, Deep Purple and Santana. After that, I learned that a friend of mine was selling an electric guitar, and I got it. My brother also played, so I asked for his approval to start playing.

"For a couple of months, I just fooled around on the guitar for half an hour or so and then set it back down in my closet. When I visited my brother in the city, he asked me if I was still playing guitar. I didn't want to tell him that I wasn't, so I said yes. He said that was great, and then suggested that we go and get some new strings for my guitar. So we went and got 'em—for five bucks of my hard-earned money—and re-strung my guitar, and that's when I really started playing.

"I started buying instructional books, but they just didn't teach what I wanted to know. So, I started listening to albums to learn. I never had much of a social life in high school, and was always kind of shy and introverted. And I never really had anything to do. So I started playing like crazy. Plus, since I idolized some of the great players so much, once I started learning their music, I felt closer to them as people. I felt I could understand them better, and that we had some sort of a spiritual relationship.

"Whenever I learn something new or write something good, I feel like I've just made **a deposit in the bank of creative ideas.**"
—*HAMMETT*

"Michael Schenker played a major role in shaping my style, and I finally got to meet him last year. I immediately told him how I learned everything he did while he was in UFO and MSG, and how I tried to get his sound by buying a Flying V, Marshalls and wah pedals. And I started to spazz out—my girlfriend had to kick me and tell me to calm down. In a weird way, to me it was like meeting Santa Claus—that's how much of an impact he had on me.

"I finally felt comfortable with my improvisation and what I was creating about three or four years into my playing. I realized that musical ideas are like seeds, and that ideas grow from other ideas. I started to see the guitar as a blank canvas, and myself as a painter. I was on to something that was creatively satisfying to me. Before then, I was always a daydreamer. The guitar was very fulfilling because it enabled me to express my daydreams musically.

"When I was younger, I thought that what I was playing was really great, and I went with that gunslinger attitude for a while. But now I realize that, back then, I was very frustrated because I hadn't reached the playing plateau that I wanted to reach. I recently realized that I've already been at that plateau for a few years, and now I've set new goals for myself—mostly in terms of being able to express myself in different ways. I'm learning the blues now like I never have before, and I'm listening to players like Albert King and Buddy Guy—guys who influenced the players who influenced me when I was younger—sort of traveling up the musical family tree.

"I feel like I've finally reached the goal that I set for myself when I was 13 or 14: to be able to play very coherently, and to say things on my guitar that I wasn't able to in normal conversation. I feel much more mature in my relationship with my instrument. Nowadays, whenever I learn something new or write something good, I feel like I've just made a deposit in the bank of creative ideas."

[8]

"People take your music and use it
in the most profound way.
And you can never think
of abusing that privilege."
—*JOE SATRIANI*

CLASS REUNION

Joe Satriani and his onetime pupil Kirk Hammett reunite for a little bit of reminiscence, a little bit of Hendrix worship and a little bit of Ice-T.

BY STEFFAN CHIRAZI

THEY ARE TWO OF ROCK'S most celebrated guitarists, but once they were teacher and student. Today, Joe Satriani and his former star pupil Kirk Hammett are old friends. Upon meeting at Hammett's spacious Berkeley, California, home, the two men exchange greetings and quickly catch up on each other's lives, the biggest news being the recent arrival of Satch's first child, Zachariah. But it doesn't take long before the focus of their conversation turns to their mutual obsessions: the guitar and, more specifically, Jimi Hendrix.

"I was only six years old when I first became aware of Hendrix," Hammett recalls. "I was probably more interested in his album covers than his music. I remember thinking that the jacket art of *Are You*

Experienced was amazing. As a kid you tend to overlook big things for silly little things."

Notes Satriani, "I just remember hearing Hendrix's music coming from one of those big Magnavox music systems, and the whole room started doing tunnel vision. I walked toward the speaker, my mouth open, and my sister asked, 'What's wrong with you?' I was totally hooked! Jimi's music completely warped my brain, and from then on I was completely pyschedelicized. It was like something happened inside of me, and I never heard anything the same after that."

"He was like [*jazz saxophonist*] John Coltrane—one of music's true innovators," adds Hammett. "He invented a whole new way of composing and recording."

"Plus, he was a snappy dresser!" injects Satriani. Hammett grins.

They adjourn to an upstairs room where, amidst a Portastudio/computer setup, the conversation begins in earnest. Out of deference to his former guru, Hammett enthusiastically volunteers to conduct the interview. Satriani immediately picks up a guitar, which he proceeds to strum, pick and pluck throughout the entire chat.

KIRK HAMMETT Joe, tell us about your early days—before the release of your first solo album, *Not of This Earth*.

JOE SATRIANI I was playing around San Francisco with a band called the Squares. We were real serious about what we were zoning in on. We thought we were really unique.

HAMMETT How much of your early material from the Squares made it onto your solo albums?

SATRIANI None of it. "Can't Slow Down" [*from* Flying in a Blue Dream] would've been a really good poppy, psychedelic, Squares-type song. We liked bands like the Gang of Four and the Police—we were influenced by anybody who did great pop. We were really prolific. If we played a song at a club on Friday and it went down badly, it was outta there, and we'd start something new in rehearsal the next day.

HAMMETT Metallica work in the opposite way. We usually start by going through tapes of riffs and rough ideas. Then we take the cream of the crop and develop them until we end up with something we like. We never throw out songs. We just hammer away until we have a finished product. What it does is leave a lot of leftover riffs, but not songs.

Joe, what are your feelings about the current guitar scene?

SATRIANI There's a lot happening right now. Anti-technique is back.

HAMMETT When you say "anti-technique," are you referring to bands like Nirvana?

SATRIANI It could be anyone in the Top Five, from Billy Ray Cyrus to Nirvana. No matter who it is, they are part of a never-ending cycle of action and reaction. But my feeling is that you shouldn't follow trends just to follow them; it's better to be 100 percent committed and dead wrong. More than likely, one day you'll find yourself on the right side if you stick with what you do.

HAMMETT I agree with that. It's better to stick to what you believe in. But getting back to the question of "technique versus anti-technique," I think one of the reasons there's this continual cycle of styles is because musicians get tired of hearing things more quickly than the public. It seems musicians are always doomed to rebel against popular trends. Guitar players in the Nineties seem to be reacting against the technique-oriented Eighties.

SATRIANI But it's too bad that guitarists feel they have to reject the whole school of technical playing. There are guitarists who reach their artistic heights through technique. Other people are just better at writing three-minute songs.

GUITAR WORLD Jamming seems to be a lost art.

HAMMETT We toured with the Black Crowes briefly in 1990, and they were the only band I'd ever seen play a blues in E for 15 minutes. I have the utmost respect for them. They played in front of a Russian audience that didn't even know how to react to any of us, and I was amazed that people really liked it. Obviously, if you go to a blues or jazz gig the fans are more accustomed to long instrumentals.

SATRIANI God, yeah. Blues fans wanna see you do it. When you play a blues gig, you really have to spill some blood!

HAMMETT I remember seeing you play a phenomenal improvised solo in concert using controlled feedback. I always wanted to compliment you on that. It's so hard to find the right spot at the right volume where a note will feed back in the right way.

SATRIANI Are you familiar with Hendrix's 1967 performance at the Monterey Pop Festival? He did the most beautiful feedback solo I've ever heard in my life! He plays a symphony there. It's just unbelievable.

A funny story from when I played with Mick Jagger on his solo Japanese tour: "Foxy Lady" was part of the set. The hardest part of playing that song is getting the opening bit of feedback to sustain properly. The only way I could do it was by kneeling down in front of a cabinet while leaning back on my toes in this really uncomfortable manner. Then I would have to wait for Mick to take it from that point. This one night I was stuck in this uncomfortable position for over a minute, looking at Mick. I was about to get desperate because I was starting to cramp, when suddenly I just fell back right into the speaker, which created a sudden *weeeeeee-BOOOMPH!* It was pretty funny. Of course, Mick had no idea what was going on; he probably thought I was just improvising or something.

GW Joe, I've heard you say that when you were teaching, you were able to see where the next generation of players was heading.

SATRIANI Oh yeah. It was very cool, because you saw things starting way before the public ever heard them. When Steve Vai was taking lessons from me, he was already beginning to work on an "Eruption"-style thing. Suddenly, I discovered lots of students messing around with tapping. Then Eddie Van Halen came along and put it all into context, adding some real dynamics and a few other elements. It was the same with you, Kirk—I heard the evolution of thrash before anyone knew what it was.

HAMMETT Remember when I introduced you to that Yngwie Malmsteen demo? I was like, "Hey Joe, check this out!" "Dark Star" was part of the demo, and we just sat there and listened to it over and over. And in two years everybody was doing it.

SATRIANI Yeah, that style was assimilated so quickly, and then it just suddenly peaked.

GW So both of you basically agree that Malmsteen did have his unique and supremely talented day.

HAMMETT He was great, but it wasn't entirely new because people like Ulrich Roth were doing it before him.

GW Kirk, what were you looking for when you took lessons from Joe?

HAMMETT How to achieve certain sounds. I used to bring him guitar solos and we'd go through them and tear them apart.

SATRIANI Kirk had a tremendous appetite for all sorts of scales, and his ear knew the differences between them.

HAMMETT We also used to discuss everyday life. When I first saw you play, I remember thinking it was a crime that you weren't making records and touring. When I saw your rise—which was pretty quick—I was very, very happy.

SATRIANI From my point of view, my rise was actually pretty slow. I recorded *Not of This Earth* between '84 and '85, using a credit card, and it didn't come out until '87. That was two years of waiting right there. I was on the edge for a long time. I had maxed out my credit card, and had no real money coming in until I joined Greg Kihn's band. [*San Francisco musician Greg Kihn had several hits in the early Eighties, most notably "Jeopardy."*] I got the call from Greg the same week the credit card company started threatening heavily. I went in, played, got some bail out money. It was funny, because whenever I played *Not of This Earth* for the band, they were thoroughly unimpressed.

Right around that time I also got an audition to join a hard rock band called Giuffria [*formed by Gregg Giuffria, formerly of the glam-metal act Angel*]. But then I realized they were this "hair" band, and I wasn't into that at all. I wanted to make that immediately clear. I had very short hair then, and when I went down there to play they were kind of cynical, too. I must've looked incredibly "Bay Area" to these L.A. guys.

So, to me, it never really seemed like a meteoric rise. When *Surfing* [with the Alien] finally became popular in 1988, I felt a mixture of achievement and relief.

HAMMETT Joe, would you say your music is spiritually driven?

SATRIANI I'm always trying to reach people with a message; it's important for me to spread something positive. I have a responsibility to get all those emotions out and across to people, from my spirit to somebody else's. For example, I could never write a song like "Cop Killer" by Body Count. That goes against everything I stand for in terms of being a performer. I couldn't go out in front of thousands of people and encourage violence.

I've been a performer for a long time. You have this power open to you: if you want people to clap their hands, they will; if you want people to shout, they will. I know I can create a domino effect of goodwill and help people get through a negative experience by confronting darker emotions.

But to go out and endorse violence in the same way you'd say "everybody put your hands together" is going beyond the limit. Why risk even one person getting killed? Is creating controversy to further your career that important? I mean, let's be honest—Kirk sells records, I sell records and so does Ice-T. But I wouldn't use that platform to spread a message like "kill the police." I mean, he can take out an ad in the *New York Times*, he can speak on public access cable TV, he can do whatever he wants. But if he gets in front of a crowd and talks about killing people...

GW Do you feel any obligation to say things onstage like, "Get out and vote?"

SATRIANI No, I don't bother with that. I just live my life as an American citizen and do my bit in my own way. When people have spent hard-earned money to come and see me play, they don't want to hear a preacher. And I don't want to be one. I come to play! I want to spread good vibes with my music. That's what Joe Satriani is all about. And to answer Kirk's question, that is how I express my spirituality. That's all I'm concerned with: making my music a deep and rich experience.

GW: Kirk, do you feel the same responsibility that Joe does?

HAMMETT Well, I think Ice-T takes it for granted that "Cop Killer" is just a song—that it's merely entertainment. I've never talked to him about it, but he's actually very mellow and very personable—which surprised the hell out of me.

SATRIANI Which makes it all the more frightening!

GW Is there a difference between Robert De Niro playing a psycho in a film and Ice-T portraying one onstage?

SATRIANI There's a big difference between being an actor and being a musician. Musicians have more responsibility because they're seen as being there just to play music, whereas it is taken for granted that an actor is a character. And do you know what? The Body Count record sucks! When that whole controversy broke, nobody reviewed the actual record. I mean it's admirable that he's trying to fuse rap and thrash, but hey, knock-knock, hello—the record sucks! Shouldn't that be the end of it? Nobody commented on the music, the songs, the performances.

Let me tell you a story. I was told about this guy, a *Flying in a Blue Dream* fanatic, who came from a troubled home. His two favorite songs were "Flying in a Blue Dream" and "I Believe." Whenever he met someone, he'd play them those songs and talk about what the music meant. These two songs were his salvation. So I guess this guy went home to finally try and confront his family problems and all that kind of stuff, and he wound up dying in a mysterious car accident. They ended up putting a tape of it in the coffin, and his whole family remembers him through "I Believe." Can you imagine what it felt like for me—sitting at home, working on guitar, looking after the baby—to hear about that?

HAMMETT We've had situations like that too. This guy's theme song was "Nothing Else Matters." He ended up dying in a car crash while he was drunk. The lyrics to "Nothing Else Matters" were put on his tombstone, which is pretty heavy.

SATRIANI The point is that people take your music and end up using it in the most profound way. And you can never think of abusing that privilege of communication between people.

GW Where does guitar go from here?

HAMMETT I think technology's going to be even more prevalent in guitar. Industrial music is getting more and more popular, as bands like Ministry and Nine Inch Nails and Godflesh are bringing computers to the forefront.

SATRIANI I agree with Kirk. But whatever style comes in vogue, there are always gonna be people who stand up and say, "That isn't soulful enough," and retain a traditional sense. Things always go in circles.

HAMMETT I think the world is ready for another Hendrix.

[**9**]

"I wanted to understand
other people's ideas about how to write lyrics."
—*JAMES HETFIELD*

BORN AGAIN

Five years have passed since Metallica
released the epic Black Album. During
that time, the music world has radically
changed—and so has Metallica.

BY TOM BEAUJOUR

"**HEN WE WERE** making our last record, nobody even knew who the fuck Kurt Cobain was!" Kirk Hammett, at ease in the lounge of the New York City recording studio where he and the rest of Metallica are rushing to finish their sixth album, *Load*, is acutely aware of how much the musical climate has changed in the five years since the band put out their last studio recording.

In the late summer of 1991, when *Metallica* was released, "smelling like teen spirit" was still something to be avoided at all costs. A few short months later, Nirvana's *Nevermind* had turned the music world on its head.

With its metallic sheen and top-dollar production values, *Metallica* (known as the Black Album to the initiated) stuck out like a sore thumb in grunge's raw sonic landscape. Yet, powered by timeless metal anthems like "Enter Sandman" and "The Unforgiven," it sold in excess of eight million copies, in the process turning Metallica into one of the biggest—if not *the* biggest—bands in the world. As it turned out, it was also heavy metal's swan song, or at least the last recording to be successfully marketed as "metal." Today, Metallica stands as the last towering monument to an era marked by bombast and excess.

When it came time to make *Load*, Metallica clearly felt the need to find a new, more forward-thinking sound. "A lot of bands get stuck staring at their own belly buttons," says vocalist/guitarist James Hetfield. "They're like, 'Wow, we made such a good record last time. We've got to keep doing this.' We won't do that. The whole point of Metallica is to come up with fresh shit."

Perhaps nothing reflects Metallica's embrace of Nineties musical values more than the band's striking new hairstyles, although both guitarists are reluctant to attribute significance to the cosmetic change: "I had fucking long hair for 20 years! Of course I cut it!" grumbles Hammett.

Metallica's new 'dos, however, are peanuts compared to the musical makeover undergone by the band. *Load* is a fiercely modern album, combining the moody melodicism of Seattle's best bands with the skull-splitting crunch that only Metallica can deliver. It's also the first album on which Hammett shares rhythm guitar duties with Hetfield.

"We wanted to get a looser sound on this record, and the best place to do that was with the guitars," Hetfield explains. "It was a little nerve-wracking at first. I felt like there was too much new shit happening in Metallica at once. And that was probably the newest thing of all, besides our stupid haircuts."

Hammett also approached the new guitar regime with a degree of trepidation. "I was actually feeling very self-conscious about it, because

I didn't want to step on James' turf," he says. "But it turned out a lot better than I thought it would, and it adds a great texture to the mix." The new division of labor, which yields slyly intertwining parts, is more closely related to the telepathic guitar interplay of the Rolling Stones than to the battering-ram riffery of Judas Priest or Diamond Head.

While amply packed with heavy fare, *Load* also finds Metallica exploring new sounds and previously unexplored genres. Songs like "2x4," with its Aerosmith-like swagger, and "Ain't My Bitch," which rocks to a ZZ Top-on-steroids groove, reflect the band's new-found ability to incorporate Hetfield's love of Southern rock and Hammett's blues jones into Metallica's patented grind. Hypnotic, pop-tinged offerings like "Hero of the Day" and "Mama Said," a startlingly lush, swirling anthem, also indicate that Hetfield has vastly expanded the emotional range of his vocal delivery. In so doing, he firmly establishes himself as one of the premier rock voices of the Nineties, along with a handful of others like Kurt Cobain, Alice in Chains' Layne Staley and Soundgarden's Chris Cornell.

And bands like Soundgarden, of which Hammett and Hetfield are both staunch admirers, are the company that Metallica intends to keep. This summer, Metallica will headline the Lollapalooza tour, sharing the bill with Cornell and company, the Ramones, Rancid and a host of other alternative rock bands. "I think that the bill on this year's Lollapalooza is pretty good," says Hammett. "It may be a little top-heavy because of us and Soundgarden, but it's certainly stronger than last year's. Fuck all those fucking elitists who say 'Metallica's not alternative' or 'They're too big of a band to play Lollapalooza.' They're just being narrow-minded."

Hetfield's take on why Metallica belongs on Lollapalooza is a bit more succinct:

"Uh, next guitar question, please."

GUITAR WORLD How long have you been working on *Load*?

JAMES HETFIELD It's been a long time, man. We started in April or May of last year. We worked on writing the songs for three or four months and just kept going and going. We had tons of material, stuff we had accumulated from five years of not writing. First it was like, "Okay, let's stop at 20 songs." Then we'd get going and say, "All right, we'll stop at 30."

It was fuckin' crazy, man. All this material had built up on the road. There were bags and bags of tapes with riffs on them. Sifting through all that shit was difficult.

GW Did you record more songs than those that are slated to appear on *Load*?

HETFIELD We recorded quite a few drum tracks, I think 28 in all. We were thinking of doing a double record, but as time went on we realized that we couldn't tackle all of it at once; we were like nine months into the recording and weren't even done with half of the songs. It was too hard to focus, too much to swallow.

GW Do you think that you'll use some of the drum tracks on your next album?

HETFIELD Oh, definitely. That'll be the next record. The tour for this album is supposed to last one year—no more. When we're done with that we'll go into the studio to finish up the 15 or 16 songs that we've already started. Hopefully, they'll still sound good to us then. If we like them, we like them; if not, we'll revamp them, add to them or do whatever it takes. But our feeling right now is that there are some good songs waiting to be finished.

> "We were like nine months into the recording and weren't even done with half of the songs. **It was too hard to focus, too much to swallow.**"
> —*HETFIELD*

GW It sounds like you're eager to accelerate your touring and recording cycle.

HETFIELD Five years between records is too crazy. We don't want to do that anymore. It's getting to be too fucking ridiculous—people waiting for new material forever, us touring too long, killing ourselves. We have to shorten these things up.

Unfortunately, it's really difficult to shorten the tours. People don't realize how global the music market has become. There didn't used to be a fucking Indonesia to play, there wasn't a South Africa, an India or a fucking Turkey. Now there is, and we want to be there. [*laughs*] We're going to have to miss a lot of places we hit on the last tour in order to be back in a year.

GW The listening public's tastes have shifted radically since you made your last album.

HETFIELD They've completely shifted since we started writing the songs for this record!

KIRK HAMMETT In the time between albums, we watched all this shit fly by and wondered, How does Metallica fit into this? And then we realized that we didn't fit into it at all, never have, and never really will.

GW Were you influenced by any of the grunge or alternative music that followed Nirvana's *Nevermind* down the pipeline?

HAMMETT The only real influence that the music I've been hearing has had is that it's sparked my interest in all the old, shitty-sounding Electro-Harmonix and MXR effects pedals I used to use when I was younger. But I listened to a lot of that Seattle stuff before it became mega-popular. When it got that big, I stopped.

HETFIELD [*to Hammett*] Why? Did they suddenly become shitty when they got popular?

HAMMETT No. I just felt that I couldn't get away from it.

HETFIELD That happened to me. When the Black Album got popular, I stopped listening to it. [*laughs*]

GW That album has sold eight million albums to date and is still on the charts. What—if any—are the drawbacks of having such a huge hit on your hands?

HETFIELD Everything gets so inflated. Everything is "More! More! More!" More touring, more interviews—more of everything. Everyone wants something—always. They can't just take you for who you are.

Luckily for us, success wasn't a night and day thing. We had taken a few steps on our way up, so we were able to handle it mentally. No one in Metallica ended up shooting himself or shooting up, or whatever it is people sometimes feel the need to do in these situations. You see it every fuckin' day in this weird-ass business.

I mean, everyone has their little things that they need to do to release pressure. When you're touring for that long, there's shit that just happens to your head. Sometimes you stray, and hopefully you've got a band that will help you through. We're really lucky to have stuck around this long without having any major crises. I mean, we've had people die in the band and things like that [*original bassist Cliff Burton was killed in a tour bus accident in 1986*], but as far as people pulling and tugging and fucking with shit, there haven't been too many problems.

It amazes me how certain bands fall apart. It's like, "Fuck, man! Can't you see that shit coming?" But sometimes they don't. It's hard to keep a band uniform and still maintain a comfortable degree of individuality; you have to respect each other all the time.

GW When you do get some time off, what do you do? Do you get as far away from music as possible?

HETFIELD I go in cycles. I won't bother listening to music for quite a while, and then I'll feel down or shitty or something and realize that it's because I haven't picked up my guitar or played music. I've conditioned myself to need this stuff for so long that I can't be away from it for too long. It's like, "Whoa, I've got to pick up the guitar and start playing." And it's scary when you haven't played for quite a while and can't remember the riff to "Seek and Destroy"!

I've noticed that it's hard to figure out what you want to do when you come off a two-year tour. While you're out on the road, you make up this list of things that you want to do when the tour's over, and then when you get home you end up vegging. It's a strange feeling to be out on your own again, not to have the Metallica family around you. There's no tour manager to wake me up and tell me to do this or that. It's like, Whoa! I have to start doing shit for myself here and deciding what I want to do. And then when I finally get it together and start doing all the shit I planned to, it's time to get back to Metallica again.

Sometimes you get torn between the two worlds. Especially when you get to our age, you start to develop a family life and get things kinda going. No one in the band is married or has kids or anything, but you have a girlfriend and your little sanctuary at home, and you've got to keep that together.

But Metallica is the fucking world to me—it always has been, and that's not going to change. Whoever becomes my partner through life has got to deal with that. I'm married to Metallica.

GW The last two Metallica albums had specific musical agendas. *...And Justice for All* (1988) was an exercise in taking the complex, challenging arrangements of *Ride the Lightning* (1984) and *Master of Puppets* (1986) to their most elaborate extreme, while *Metallica* was an exercise in economy...

HETFIELD Economy, my ass! [*laughs*] That was the most expensive record we've ever made.

GW ...in which you reigned in your song structures and focused on crafting more concise rock songs. What were your goals for this album?

HETFIELD We wanted to attain a certain degree of looseness with this record. The drums are pretty much as anal as ever, but the vocals, and particularly the guitars, breathe a lot more. Instead of me playing all of the rhythm guitars and trying to double them as closely as possible, like I'd done on our previous albums, both Kirk and I play contrasting rhythm parts on almost all of the record. There isn't really much of that one-dimensional wall of heavy guitar—with a clean guitar coming in once in a while—that we've had on previous albums. I wanted a "medium" sound, if there is such a thing. I was like, "How do I get that? I fucking don't know."

GW Was it decided before you began recording that both of you would play rhythm guitar on this album?

HAMMETT No. It was never really something that we spoke about. The first mention of it came while we were recording the drum tracks. When we do that, we all play the songs together in a single room, but the only thing that goes onto the multi-track is the drums—everything else just gets taped. Some of the songs were sounding so good on those tapes that James was like, "Well, maybe Kirk should play on the final version of some of these."

Later on, on a day when James happened to be away on a hunting trip, I was laying down a couple of solos, and when I finished the lead on one of the tunes, our producer, Bob Rock, said, "Okay, tune up and we'll do the rhythm for this song now." I was like, "What?"

HETFIELD By the time I came back, Kirk had put down rhythm tracks on four songs.

HAMMETT I specifically went out of my way to come up with a second guitar part that would complement James', not ape it. Not that the riffs weren't interesting. The riffs are the riffs—they're the most important part of the song.

Our parts have a really good sense of interplay. And you can actually separate the two guitars and tell who's playing what. James is on the left side, and I'm on the right.

GW James, was it difficult for you to surrender control?

HAMMETT I don't think it's a control issue as much as it used to be. It's more that we're all here to accomplish a common goal.

HETFIELD It was what was needed for the record. The looseness just wasn't coming across. No matter how many fucking martinis I had, I could never get the guitar tracks to sound different enough. It was the same guitar player playing it fucked up. It wasn't a fucked-up guitar player trying to play it right. [*laughs*]

Basically, no matter how close Kirk plays the riff to the way I did, it won't sound the same because it's his fingers, his style and his attitude. I would lay a basic scratch track of what I thought the other guitar should be, and Kirk would come in, listen to the track and then do his own thing with it, which was cool.

GW In the past, was the fact that Kirk didn't get to play rhythm guitar on the records a source of tension within the band?

HAMMETT Not really. In fact, on this album we argued more about the solos than anything else. But we're always arguing about something, so it was just par for the course.

HETFIELD I often have a pretty specific idea of what the solo to a particular song should sound like, so it throws me for a loop when Kirk comes in with something else. But then everyone sits down, we talk it out and work out a middle ground that everyone can be happy with.

You don't want to have something on a record that someone in the band is going to go insane over and hate.

HAMMETT We try and resolve things right away, so that two years from now no one will say something sarcastic to the other person about it.

HETFIELD Well, they probably will anyway. But at least there won't be too much fuel behind it.

GW What were the bones of contention?

HETFIELD "Is that in key? Are you sure that's in key?" [*laughs*]

HAMMETT I had to sit down and explain my approach. I probably have the most open mind of anyone in Metallica, as far as music is concerned. I like a lot of different stuff and so, occasionally, I'll take an idea inspired by something sort of "out" and bring it to the band. I won't bring it to the band unless I think that there's a chance that they'll like it, and 90 percent of the time they do. But there's that 10 percent of the time where they question it.

On this album, there was one song—which will remain nameless to protect the innocent—where the solo that I played had such a different type of feel that it changed that entire piece of the song. We spent hours debating it, and I literally had to walk James through every single note. There was something about it that he just didn't like, which he thought might have been a harmonic thing. But then we realized that it was just the general sound of the solo. Then James came up with something—like five notes—that colored what I had played sufficiently to make it work for him too.

GW Your solos on this album are very textured.

HAMMETT I would hate to say that I'm bored with the standard rock guitar solo, but I've done it for five albums now, and this time I wanted to go in a completely different direction. I wasn't interested in showing off any more. I wanted to play something that fit the song more like a part than a solo per se, something that had the power to establish a completely different mood in the section of the song that was allocated to me.

When I play at home, I have a Lexicon Jam Man sampling delay with which I can create loops on which to layer guitar textures. That's why things like the Roland VG-8 and the guitar synth are so interesting to me—they put so many sounds at my disposal.

Don't get me wrong, though, I still listen to Jimi Hendrix, Stevie Ray Vaughan, Buddy Guy, Robert Fripp and Adrian Belew. I'm still way into that type of guitar playing. I just don't feel the need to play that way within the context of Metallica any more.

GW You've also almost abandoned your wah pedal, which you used on most of the solos on the last album.

HAMMETT I didn't notice that until just the other day. I was laying down a wah track and I said to Bob, "Guess what? We don't have the problem we had on the last album. You don't have to hide the wah pedal anymore."

GW The slide solo on "Ain't My Bitch" is a first for you.

HAMMETT We wanted to find something different for that song, not just another guitar solo. The slide was really effective because it's such a new sound for us. It's only recently that I've felt comfortable enough with my slide work to actually commit to playing it on the record. I've been working on it for years now—it's not an easy thing to do. I'm actually really proud of that guitar solo.

GW Do you use any open tunings when you play slide?

HAMMETT Man, that shit just confuses me. When I found out that Duane Allman used standard tuning, it really inspired me to work on my slide chops. Before that, I thought that slide players all worked in open G and could use all the tricky tunings.

GW The solo on "Bleeding Me" also sounds particularly inspired.

HAMMETT That's the one lead that I played totally off-the-cuff. I did seven or eight passes, and it felt so goddamn good. Every time I finished a take, Bob would look at me and say, "Wow!" It's one of the more typical "rock" solos on the album. I had the wah pedal going, and I was going for a combination of fast playing and long, sustained notes. It has everything in there: melody, hooks, rock and roll phrasing, a bluesy vibe, lots of dynamics, and the Hendrixisms that I always try to sneak in there.

GW James, you also play quite a bit of lead guitar on *Load*.

HETFIELD Honest to goodness, I don't know anymore. So much different shit has gone on this record as far as laying guitar tracks that I kind of forget what actually made it into the final mix.

HAMMETT I don't feel as possessive about the guitar parts as I have in the past, precisely because there's so much there. I mean, ultimately it doesn't really matter who played what; the parts are just there to make the songs happen. I mean, at this point, I think that people know we can play.

GW All of *Load* is tuned down a half step—another first for you.

HETFIELD Tuning down a half step helped a lot of things, like getting the bends going in the riffs. The most fun thing in the world is sitting down with your guitar tuned down a whole step and riffing out. Unfortunately, that sounds too muddy, so we settled for tuning down a half step. Tuning down also helps me a lot by extending the apparent range of my voice.

GW Vocally, you've taken a lot of chances with this album.

HETFIELD I feel that it's more raw. It was a lot more fun doing the vocals this time, not as stiff a process. We were trying to be a little less anal.

GW In the past, though, Metallica has always been a band that holds itself to an extreme level of studio perfection.

HETFIELD There's still that. There's still a desire for perfection, but this time we let little things go. If the verdict was, "Well, that thing you sang was a bit pitchy, but it has some major attitude," then fuck it, let it ride.

On *Metallica*, the vocals were so in the pocket all the time. I was trapped by the fact that I forced myself to repeat certain phrases exactly every time they occurred within a song.

GW Did you go so far as to use vocal sampling on the last album, to ensure that recurring parts would be exactly the same?

HETFIELD Well, there were a couple of times where we flew in the background vocals on a chorus or something—just to save the time doing the donkey work. But I didn't feel right about doing even that this time. I sang everything.

GW On "Poor Twisted Me," your vocals are distorted. Is there an industrial music influence creeping in there?

HETFIELD We wanted to get some different sounds. That's just a good old Shure bullet mic, usually used for harmonica. It's got a distinct sound that you can't do too much to, but it's pretty cool for what it is.

But I wouldn't call that an industrial sound or anything. It's just a mic being used for an application it wasn't designed for. The song called out for it. I had always told myself, "I'm never ever going to use that distorted vocal sound that everyone uses." But it fit lyrically.

I've been really focusing on lyricists—as opposed to people who just sit down and crank out some words for a song—who write fucking poems and then put music to them. I wanted to understand other people's ideas about how to write lyrics. Nick Cave's *Murder Ballads* is the coolest, and I dig all the Tom Waits stuff. I've even listened to some Leonard Cohen. I mean, I hate the fucking music, but his lyrics are very cool.

GW You do a lot more "acting" with your singing.

HETFIELD The way we recorded the vocals this time made it a bit easier, not exactly to get into character, but to feel the vocals a bit more than before. All the other times I did vocals, I sat in front of some expensive microphone—stranded out in the cold fucking tracking room. There always was a big X on the floor, and I wasn't allowed to move from that spot.

This time I thought, You know, I have a great time with the vocals in my studio at home. I fuck around with them and they come out fine. Why can't we try that here? So we'd take the SM-57 or whatever mic we were using and I would walk around the control room and just yell—and it was fine. It was very liberating not having to worry about where I had to stand and all this other bullshit. I could just worry about what I was singing.

GW Apparently, Henry Rollins does much the same thing when he's cutting vocals. He actually has to tape the headphones to his head because he gets so animated.

HETFIELD Fuck headphones, man! We had the big fatties [*large studio monitors*] cranked. There's a little bleed, but fuck it. You've got to go for vibe.

GW Earlier you referred to "a lot of changes happening in Metallica." What, besides the changes in your rhythm guitar approach—and your haircuts—were you referring to?

HETFIELD In general, there's a looser attitude. Some new things happened with Jason [*Newsted, bassist*]. In the past, Lars [*Ulrich, drummer*] and I had the fucking shackles on everybody. This time, if we came into the studio and heard Jason laying down some slap bass part on a song, we'd be like, "What the fuck? Okay, let's count to 10 and hear it in the context of the song. We're open-minded here." It was difficult at times.

I had noticed over the years how frustrated Jason was musically and how a lot of the stuff he'd written wasn't getting onto the records. It also used to really bug me that he was jamming with all of these other bands. He'd make a demo with some friends, and somehow it would end up on the radio and I'd be like, "What the fuck are you doing, Jason? This is Metallica! You can't do that shit!" Then I realized that he was doing it because he needs to get his shit out. He wants people to hear his stuff.

HAMMETT It's a good creative outlet and completely healthy for him. And ultimately, what's healthy for him is healthy for us.

HETFIELD We kept his frustration in mind while we hashed out the parts he put down on the record.

GW Are there specific things on *Metallica* that you wanted to improve on *Load*?

HAMMETT The one thing that strikes me about *Metallica* when I go back and listen to it is that there isn't enough variation in my tone. I kind of stuck with the same sound, and the only variation was a wah pedal here and a wah pedal there, or the minimal tonal variation that you get from tuning down.

But you can't really look back. If you do, you end up constantly comparing yourself to the past, and that has a way of holding you back. You end up with a whole catalog of albums that sound like one particular album that was successful. The idea should be to move forward and try and develop a new vision.

GW You did, however, keep one important part of the Metallica formula intact when you decided to work with Bob Rock again.

How has your relationship with him developed?

HETFIELD When we started working on *Metallica*, Bob was much more passive than he is now. He was afraid to take control. Now our relationship goes through phases, depending on what needs to be done. At different times, Bob tries to exert a little more authority over us. We laugh at him and move on. [*laughs*]

HAMMETT The thing with Bob is that he can read us pretty well at this point—he definitely knows what we're capable of. I know that on this album I came in and did a really great job at what I had to do, and a lot of that was the result of him zoning on a particular idea that I had and him telling me to build on it. Then there have been times where I've been a bit hungover and not happening, and he's flown off the handle and yelled, "Get your shit together!"

> "Bob can read us pretty well at this point—he definitely knows what we're capable of."
> —*HAMMETT*

But you know what—and I probably shouldn't say this—there have been times when I've come in hungover and been able to play really well. And I think that in a few of those situations, being hung over has added a certain edge to my playing.

HETFIELD [*laughs*] Oh no!

HAMMETT I'm not advocating drinking, and this is a highly personal point of view, but there has been the occasional session where I've come in a little hung over—not super hung over—and it's made me think more and feel a little more sensitive to the needs of the track.

HETFIELD Kids, don't try this at home.

HAMMETT But getting back to Bob, I think that he's really good at coaching us through things.

HETFIELD That's his gig. He's not here to tell us what to do. He's trying to get the best shit he can out of us all the time.

He's also a really solid guitar player with a good knowledge of theory, which can be really helpful in a bind. I'll be trying to work out a harmony, and he'll come in and say, "Well, A is the relative minor of blah blah blah," and since I don't know any of that shit, it's nice to have the instruction booklet right next to me.

HAMMETT He's always pulling out the relative minor. It's his favorite thing.

GW *Load* has much more of an in-your-face mix than *Metallica*, which had considerable amounts of ambiance in the mix.

HETFIELD I wanted the guitars back in your face again. I like the way *Kill 'Em All* just had fucking guitars up your ass and the drums were not the leader of the group. I think that on the Black Album, everyone wanted to be up-front. But something has to be back there, and it ended up being the guitars, which were given a wider, thinner sound and pushed back. I think that on this album, the drums drive the rhythm instead of leading the band, and there are these two guitars playing different things right up front.

I had one big fear when we went to the two guitar player thing: "Is the fucking riff still going to be heard?" That's always been really important in this group. But I think we found a nice balance between them, and their level in the mix was crucial.

GW Were you asked to play Lollapalooza? Or did you do the asking?

HETFIELD They asked us. We thought about it and said, "All right, why the fuck not?" All it is is a European style rock festival. We've done festivals all over the world.

HAMMETT It's like the Reading Festival [*an annual British festival*]— except that it moves from place to place. We're used to being on different bills with different people. I mean, we played one festival in Belgium where we shared the bill with Neil Young, Lenny Kravitz, Sugar, Sonic Youth, the Levelers and the Black Crowes. That would never happen in America because those bands mean something completely different over here than they do in Europe.

The whole impetus behind Lollapalooza was to do something different and challenging. And I think that the bill with us on it is different and challenging—more recently, they were stuck in a rut where they had to have alternative bands and indie bands.

GW Is it true that you played an important role in selecting the bands for this year's lineup?

HAMMETT We did and we didn't. A lot of it had to do with availability. A lot of bands that we wanted were touring on their own. I mean, I would have liked to have Al Green or the Cocteau Twins.

HETFIELD We're not picking Lollapalooza. We're not coming in to take it over. We're just gonna play. We don't really want to have anything to do with Lollapalooza except play it.

GW Are you looking forward to seeing any of the bands that will be on the bill with you.

HAMMETT I like the vibe of Lollapalooza. I've been to every single one; I've actually jammed at a few, too. When Ministry was out I played with them a few times, and I did the same with Primus. I've fucking loved Soundgarden since '85 or '86. And everyone loves the Ramones. I was talking to Johnny Ramone the other day and he was saying, "Goddamn it Kirk, I'd already be retired and playing golf in L.A. if it wasn't for you guys calling us up and asking us to do this summer tour." And I said, "Well Johnny, there isn't any better way to go."

[10]

"There was a time when we thought
that Metallica was a very strict family
and **anything outside of
Metallica was pretty
much prohibited.**"
—*KIRK HAMMETT*

COVER STORY

Who says playing in a cover band sucks?
Back in 1998, Metallica played the heavy hits and
killed 'em all with *Garage Inc.*, their two-disc
collection of the songs that inspired them.

BY JEFF KITTS

IT'S A CHILLY AUGUST NIGHT at the Shoreline Amphitheater, a cavernous outdoor monstrosity—actually, a former landfill—just outside San Francisco. The 40,000 or so in attendance are primed and ready to receive the full-bore heavy metal onslaught of their lives. Sizzling opening sets by Jerry Cantrell and Days of the New have kept the energy level at a proper feverish pitch. Finally, the stage lights dim, a roar shoots skyward, and hysteria reigns supreme. As their customary *The Good, the Bad and the Ugly* theme song intro fades out, Metallica bound onto the stage and launch headlong into... "Breadfan"? Many in the crowd look perplexed and are clearly unfamiliar with the song.

And that's hardly surprising. Not only has "Breadfan" never appeared on a Metallica album—it's not even an official Metallica song. It was written in the early Seventies by a British rock band called Budgie. So what is the band doing, shocking the hometown faithful by opening with an unknown song?

"It's just good to fuck with people, that's all," Metallica frontman James Hetfield says afterward, referring to the band's opening salvo. "The first song of the set is always the 'Yeah, dude, all right!' song of the night, and when we come out with a cover, you can tell that a lot of people don't recognize it. There's this machismo thing where guys don't want to admit to their buddies that they don't know the song. But hopefully they'll find out from someone what the song was and go discover the band that wrote it."

For more than 15 years now, Metallica have ruled the roost. Few could argue that the core of the band's spectacular success has been their songs. But while original compositions like "For Whom the Bell Tolls," "Master of Puppets," "One" and "Enter Sandman" are the hard rocks upon which Metallica stand, James Hetfield, Kirk Hammett et al have always been a formidable cover band as well. Die-hard fans have cherished Metallica's versions of little-known British heavy metal classics like "Breadfan," the Anti-Nowhere League's crazed "So What" and Diamond Head's "Am I Evil?"

Despite the band's relatively casual approach to them in the studio, cover songs were always taken seriously by Metallica. On the one hand, they regarded the covers, which were mostly of older tunes, as a way of staying in touch with their own metal and punk rock roots. Metallica also saw them as a means of paying tribute to the original artists—usually obscure British bands—who inspired them during their formative years. Most were short, speedy songs teeming with the kind of pure, raw power and attitude not always found in the band's later recordings.

"Our older covers definitely have a certain rough charm," Hammett says, "because we didn't put them under a microscope or record them as anally as we would normally record our own songs."

Nevertheless, recording cover songs has always been serious business for Metallica, a way of staying in touch with their metal and punk rock roots. Throughout their career they've recorded close to 20 covers, issuing them primarily as B-sides of singles. In 1987, following the death of original bassist Cliff Burton and subsequent hiring of Jason Newsted, the band issued a five-song collection of covers called *The $5.98 E.P.: Garage Days Re-Revisited*. The record, meant as a gift to the band's hardcore fans, was taken out of print soon after its release, making it one of the most sought-after Metallica collectibles.

Having each of these songs in one complete package is something Metallica fans have repeatedly wished for—but the longing stops here. Coming in late November will be a new two-CD set from Metallica, *Garage Inc.*, complete with every cover song they've ever recorded—including Queen's "Stone Cold Crazy," Motörhead's "Overkill" and Diamond Head's "The Prince," plus the entire contents of the *Garage Days* record.

In addition to the five rare *Garage Days* tracks, including "Helpless" (Diamond Head), "The Small Hours" (Holocaust) and "Crash Course in Brain Surgery" (Budgie), and each of the songs mentioned previously, the new album will feature a mix of newly recorded covers that pay homage to other bands that have impacted the Metallica sound through the years. Some groups, like Black Sabbath, Thin Lizzy and the Misfits, are not unexpected, while others, like Bob Seger, seem out of character. But the point is that it is in character. Metallica have always been comfortable hurling the occasional curve ball at their audience. As far as they're concerned, anything goes when it comes to picking cover songs—well, almost.

"You can pick up a very shitty song to cover," says Hetfield. "I mean, the Foo Fighters doing 'Baker Street'? I don't get that at all. It does take me back to high school, I guess, or at least to a song that I completely fucking hated." He laughs. "So you have to be careful."

"Back then **we had one volume and one speed.** That was it."
—*HETFIELD*

GUITAR WORLD Let's talk about some of the new cover songs that will appear on this album.

KIRK HAMMETT We're doing a Black Sabbath song called "Sabbra Cadabra," which was on *Sabbath Bloody Sabbath*. It's that opening riff that just really gets us going—it's such a jamming riff. We might try to glue "Sabbra Cadabra" together with another Sabbath song, but we haven't figured that out yet. We'll also be doing a Misfits song called "Die, Die My Darling," a nice little ditty we've been listening to for the last 15 years or so. There will also be a Bob Seger song called "Turn the Page." It's a very odd choice; I'm not a big Bob Seger fan. But "Turn the Page" is a great song about being on the road. It's kind of ballady, but when you hear it, you can really picture James singing it.

There's also a Mercyful Fate medley. Their stuff was so incredibly heavy and progressive for its time. Their guitarists, Hank Shermann and Michael Denner, wrote some of the best riffs of all time. Musically, they came from the same place that we did: old UFO, Iron Maiden, Diamond Head, Motörhead, Judas Priest, Tygers of Pan Tang. Fate had an incredibly huge influence on us in the early days. The other night we were rehearsing the medley, and Lars said, "Man, this stuff sounds like us!" We'll also be doing Thin Lizzy's version of "Whiskey in the Jar," an old Irish drinking song. Cliff turned me on to Thin Lizzy's *Night Life* album; I had always listened to albums like *Bad Reputation*, *Jailbreak* and *Renegade*, but I was never really familiar with that album until Cliff turned me on to it. There will also be a couple of Discharge tunes.

GW Will you be re-recording any of the older cover material?

HETFIELD No, although we will remaster everything so at least all the volume levels will be the same. [*laughs*] But we want to keep that kind of dated sound with some of that material. It's the sound of our history.

GW Is the band always conscious of being faithful to the original versions when you record covers?

HETFIELD More so in the early days. I think a lot of that, particularly with the older covers, was because we really didn't know that we had our own style. We were inspired by those songs, so we played them like the original versions. But now we have our own style, so we know how to manipulate a song, and we know what we can and can't do. Back then we had one volume and one speed. That was it.

HAMMETT Our attitude now is, whatever the song needs, we'll do. We're going to take as much liberty as we want to with these new songs. We're gonna screw around with the arrangements, change guitar parts, even change guitar riffs if it suits us. We'll also be shifting around a lot of keys, which is something we've never really done before. With our own material, once something is in a certain key, it's committed to that key—it doesn't really change. But with these songs,

we're moving stuff from C♯ to E or from E to C♯ or from G to F♯—
whatever feels right. Shifting keys might make something easier for
James to sing, or allow us to get some open-string resonation going.
Or maybe we'll tune something down just to make it heavier. We're
just taking these songs to wherever we feel they must be taken.

GW What factors into the process of picking cover songs?

HETFIELD There has to be something there initially for us to like
and want to cover it. It might be the riff, the beat, or even the lyric—but it's never all three. [*laughs*] Sometimes you have this song
with a great riff, and when you finally chase down the lyrics you
read them and go, "What the fuck? Man, I liked it better when I
didn't know the lyrics." [*laughs*] Or you have a great lyric and the
riff is like...hmmm. There were a few Budgie songs where all of a
sudden they went into some hippy-trippy mellow bit in the middle,
and we said, "Well, either we have to make fun of it or just fucking
forget that part."

GW Do you remember what originally influenced the band to play
covers in your early days?

HETFIELD Like any other band starting out, we would cover songs
because we needed to have enough songs to fill up the set when we
played live. We had "Hit the Lights," "The Four Horsemen" and a few
others, but not enough originals to do a full set. And since we were
covering songs by these British heavy metal bands, people thought
they were our own songs.

GW What motivated you to record cover songs?

HAMMETT Basically, it was a good way for us to warm up and get the
feel of the studio when we went in to record an album.

GW How did you discover bands like Diamond Head and Budgie and
the whole New Wave of British Heavy Metal?

HETFIELD Lars. He introduced me to a whole new world of heavy music. I was more into bands like Black Sabbath, Thin Lizzy, Aerosmith, AC/DC, Ted Nugent, Kiss, et cetera. I had heard of Iron Maiden and Def Leppard, but not too many of the other, more obscure, English metal bands. So when I first met up with Lars, I would spend days just going through his record collection, taping over my REO Speedwagon cassettes with bands like Angel Witch and Diamond Head and Motörhead. I was in heaven at his house.

HAMMETT It was pretty much the same thing with me. When I met Lars, I was just amazed at how much he knew about European metal. I knew about all the major bands and was into most of the same stuff he and James were, but Lars knew so much about all the more obscure bands like Parallax and Witchfynde and Quartz.

GW How did these bands specifically influence Metallica?

HETFIELD Diamond Head, for example, had a pretty unique way of putting songs together. It wasn't the traditional verse-chorus-verse-chorus–middle eight and then out; they had middle breakdowns, new riffs that came in at weird places, and their songs kind of took you on journeys. Budgie and Mercyful Fate were also pretty inventive. Fate would play a great riff and never come back to it and it would piss you off. [*laughs*] But those bands taught us that there were more than three parts to a song—that you could have a song with different parts, each of which could almost be its own song.

You can really hear their impact on *...And Justice for All*, which was where we really started to go over the top with that type of song-writing. Sometimes we look back at a lot of our material and wonder how—or why—we ever came up with certain parts. Or wonder why we just didn't turn certain riffs into their own songs, because they were so good. We went out drinking one night recently, and on our long ride to this club, we listened to a radio station playing Metallica from A to Z. And it was really wild to hear some of our old material again. When they'd play something like "The Frayed Ends of Sanity," from ...*And Justice for All*, we'd sit there and go, "Whoa! Where in the fuck did that whole middle section come from? What were we thinking?" There was a lot of urgency to that material, but a lot of it was just wank— just us showing off. But that's where we were at that time.

"A lot of it for us is covering songs out of respect. Here's a band that helped us out, and in our way we're helping them out now."

—*HETFIELD*

GW Is that different from where the band is right now?

HETFIELD Oh, absolutely. It's also different from where we originally started. Back then, it was just about writing these *bam!*, hit-you-kinda-quick songs, then we got into the longer epic-y things. On the Black Album, we started to trim up again and get a little more to the point.

GW Does playing covers, particularly older ones like "Breadfan," ever bring you back to an earlier time, a time when you didn't have every-thing you have today?

HETFIELD Like a baby in a trailer at the Shoreline Amphitheater? [*laughs*] No, it really doesn't take me back. For me, it's always now. Whether we're doing a cover song or "Fight Fire with Fire" live, this is how we play it now. I know how we played it on the record and I know the initial thought behind the song, but this is how we feel now. And even with our own material, as you play it you add new things, stuff that makes you feel good now, or stuff that you can play that you couldn't back then. It's always "now" for us. As far as the lyrics, some of them take on new meanings as you get older; others just become sounds that come out of your mouth.

What really takes me back is watching our old videos. I recently saw the "Nothing Else Matters" video, which was us recording in the studio, and it was really weird for me. It wasn't really that long ago, but we sure looked a lot different then. [*laughs*] So we can get a little nostalgic here and there.

GW Is it gratifying to expose bands like Diamond Head and Budgie to a larger audience?

HETFIELD We don't really look at it that way. The way it works out is, here's a band that helped us out, and in our way we're helping them out now. It's not intentional, but that's the way it turns out. A lot of it for us is covering songs out of respect.

When we went to Lemmy's 50th birthday party [*held at the Whisky a Go Go in Los Angeles in December 1995*] and played a bunch of Motörhead songs dressed as four Lemmys, we did that out of sheer respect. I mean, he's the godfather of heavy metal, and the truth is that he inspired me to sing and play in an aggressive style. So it's all about respect.

I'm not saying it's because of us, but you take a band like Holocaust, and suddenly, after all these years, they've reformed and gone out on tour—and that's kinda cool. Take Diamond Head. They supported us at a gig in England a few years back, and they hadn't played together for years. And I don't want to say who, but there have certainly been bands through the years that have asked us to cover their songs, but we won't do it because of that.

But you know, the same has happened to us in some ways. The Mighty Mighty Bosstones once did a cover of "Enter Sandman" on an album [*1992's* Where'd You Go?] and that might have helped us gain exposure in the ska underground. And then you have Apocalyptica [*a string quartet from Finland known for covering Metallica songs*]. Even Pat Boone did a Metallica cover [*"Enter Sandman" on 1997's* In a Metal Mood].

GW In 1987 the band recorded an entire record of cover songs, the *$5.98 E.P.—Garage Days Re-Revisited*, which was taken out of print soon after its release. How did that record happen?

HETFIELD We were still dealing with Cliff's death, and Q-Prime, our management, was telling us to jump right back into it and start playing again. Obviously, when you deal with a death, you want to take some mourning time, but our management pushed us a bit to get going again. I guess we kind of mourned through music and doing the cover songs on that album.

HAMMETT Doing that album was also a good way for us to break Jason in to the public and give our audience a preview of what was to come. We needed to buy some time, because we really weren't ready to record another full-length album yet. We didn't have anything new written. So it was a good way for us to put some product out there and take our time before getting ready to do *...And Justice for All.*

GW A whole new generation of Metallica fans have grown up that are unfamiliar with Cliff Burton. What are some of your best memories of him?

HAMMETT Well, I roomed with him, so I spent more time with him than the other guys. Cliff had a lot of music in him that never had the chance to come out. He was always listening to music or

> "Cliff had his own unique voice, musically, and I definitely think there was a part of the Metallica sound that was **lost forever when he died."**
> —*HAMMETT*

playing music—I mean constantly. Toward the last four or five months of his life, he started playing a lot more guitar. He'd single out little licks or riffs when he listened to music and would have me figure them out for him. I remember him really loving the way Ed King of Lynyrd Skynyrd played guitar. He'd always ask me to show him Skynyrd licks, and then he'd end up saying, "Man, that's tricky. That's really tricky." [*laughs*] And he loved Black Sabbath and Creedence Clearwater Revival. And the Misfits, Thin Lizzy, Sex Pistols, Velvet Underground and the Eagles. Oh, he used to drive me crazy with the Eagles.

Cliff really knew a lot about music theory. I remember him playing me these volume-swell things that he had come up with and that we later used as the intro to "Damage, Inc.," from *Master of Puppets*. He told me it was based on some Bach piece, and that it had a death theme to it, some funeral march thing. When I listened to it after his death, I always found that pretty ironic. He used to carry around a nylon string classical guitar that was detuned to C#! I once asked him why it was detuned, and he said, "So I can bend the strings." [*laughs*]

GW Were you able to learn from him as a musician?

HAMMETT Oh, absolutely. All the harmony stuff that I know and that James knows basically came from Cliff. I knew about harmony, but I really didn't know how to apply it. But Cliff did. He wrote all the harmony parts for the whole last part of "Orion," from *Master of Puppets*. He would sit down with us and map out harmonies on paper, like, "Okay, it's in the key of E, so you've got your root note here, and we'll go a fifth here," or, "Now we're going to a G, so let's put a major third here," and he'd write it all down.

GW What was the band's mindset after Cliff's death?

HAMMETT Such a huge void was created after he died—a really big hole that only he could fill. I worried that we'd never find anyone else like him, but then I realized that we shouldn't even try. He was just one of a kind. He really had his own unique voice, musically, and I definitely think there was a part of the Metallica sound that was lost forever when he died.

HETFIELD But that was why finding Jason was kind of a whole new inspiration in itself for us—just getting this new blood in the band really helped us move on. And [*grinning*] he was so fucking excited to be in the band, it was almost embarrassing.

GW Lately, we've been hearing rumors that Jason hasn't been particularly happy as a member of Metallica. Is there any truth to that?

HAMMETT No, no, everything's really cool with Jason. More so now than any time before. We've given him a lot more space to stretch out and pursue his own individual things. There was a time when we thought that Metallica was a very strict family and anything outside of Metallica was pretty much prohibited. But we've all kind of matured, and now we realize that it really doesn't have to be that way. We've let loose a bit on the reins, and Jason's been able to go out and do his own thing. But he's still very much a part of Metallica.

GW It must have been tough for him, coming in as Cliff's replacement.

HAMMETT Yeah. There was a lot of grief and a lot of anguish when Cliff died, and basically Jason was the punching bag. We vented so much on Jason because of the whole bus accident and Cliff's death, and it really wasn't fair to do that to him. But things are different nowadays. Our relationship with him is much more comfortable.

[*At this point Hammett grabs his '53 Strat and heads off to tape a lesson with* Guitar World's *Nick Bowcott. Back in the trailer, James and I open a discussion about his development as the band's lyricist.*]

GW Lyrically speaking, it's highly unlikely that you would ever write a song like the Misfits' "Last Caress" or the Anti-Nowhere League's "So What," with its verse, "I fucked a sheep, I fucked a goat, I rammed my cock right down its throat."

HETFIELD That's kind of the cool thing. It's just so much fun to get up there and sing, "I've even sucked an old man's cock" and watch people in the audience go, Huh? It's just shit that shocks people, and I can go, "Hey, I didn't write it." [*laughs*]

"Writing specifically about women is something that, **for us, is kind of taboo.**"
—*HETFIELD*

"So What" was actually a song that we'd throw on the stereo in the early days just to piss off the neighbors. Whether they could hear the lyrics or not, it just felt good to blast the words "cock" and "fuck" and stuff like that. And that was absolutely why we chose to cover it. It wasn't because it had some great riff or something. [*laughs*]

GW Metallica are usually so serious. It must be a release to sing something absurd.

HETFIELD There is a great positive to that, but the negative side comes when the lyrics are really stupid and you can't get into them. It's hard to project and be convincing when that happens.

GW Looking back, how do you feel about your lyrics on *Kill 'Em All*?

HETFIELD They were where our heads were at, so they were absolutely right, because that was how we felt. And I wouldn't change anything about them. Just the honesty and the innocence of it all is so cool. It's all we knew at the time: "bang your head," "crush the town" and all that shit.

GW Can you still relate to that now?

HETFIELD Absolutely. The cool thing about Metallica and our history is that there's always a new generation of angry young men who latch onto *Kill 'Em All* and know what I'm talking about, and maybe they grow up with the rest of the records. We've never been about creating some fantasy world with our records; we're just documenting where we're at, at the time. There's always going to be youth on the planet, and whether they can relate to that or not, I don't know. But every time I look out in the crowd and see some kids battling it out in the middle of the mosh pit, I'm like, Yeah, I was there, man.

GW How do you view *Kill 'Em All* in terms of your skill as a lyricist?

HETFIELD I guess there was some thought put into it. I mean, at least they rhymed. [*laughs*] At the time I couldn't write a lyric to save my life, so all I could do was listen to other bands and see how they phrased things. I just wanted to put our attitude into it, and that's why I loved punk at the time. It was that honesty, which is something I'm not sure a lot of the older metal bands had. I mean, what was Judas Priest really writing about? Or Iron Maiden? It was all this weird fantasy stuff. And we maybe got into a little of that with "Phantom Lord" or a few other songs, but we've always tried to stay away from writing about things we didn't know about.

GW How did you manage to avoid falling into that heavy metal trap of writing about dungeons and dragons?

HETFIELD I think we realized early on just how goofy it was. Those lyrics didn't mean anything to me; they just didn't pump me up. What did pump me up were punk rock lyrics, stuff that I could maybe relate to or that would give me a little attitude. For the listener, those lyrics are about feeling comfortable knowing that the guy who wrote them is just as fucked up as you are. There's some kind of kinship in that.

GW You also tend to avoid writing about women in your songs.

HETFIELD Actually, the word "she" appears in a couple of our songs... but it's usually about murdering her, so it's okay. [*laughs*] But truthfully, "Nothing Else Matters" is a song that was kind of influenced by a woman, but it also pertains to everyone. I've always found that it works quite a bit better when you have a certain vagueness to it, even though you know what the initial inspiration was behind the lyrics. But yes, writing specifically about women is something that, for us, is kind of taboo, mainly because it's been done to death and, to be honest, it's kind of silly. To me, if you're gonna write about a woman, there are other ways to do it.

You know, a lot of times, lyrics really don't matter all that much. But as the lyricist, when I write something, I want it to be the best that it can be.

GW On *Ride the Lightning*, you began dealing with more personal and social issues, among them suicide [*"Fade to Black"*] and capital punishment [*"Ride the Lightning"*]. What caused you to mature as a lyricist?

HETFIELD Touring definitely made us a little more worldly, even if it was just hopping in the Winnebago with [*early Eighties British metallers*] Raven and touring across the country. [*laughs*] We started to see other things that were going on in the world. And that's when more of the punk-oriented, opinionated kind of thoughts began to appear in our lyrics. It was about putting yourself in other people's shoes: what if this were to happen to you? Just creating different scenarios.

And actually having to sit down and write an album made a difference, because *Kill 'Em All* was just songs that we had been playing in clubs for the two years before we recorded it. Getting

Cliff in the band also made a difference when it came to writing these songs, because he was more of an educated musician and, along with the music, we felt we had to at least be a little more educated lyrically.

GW The song "Ride the Lightning" appears to sympathize with the criminal in the electric chair. Was that an anti–capital punishment statement?

HETFIELD Not exactly. I believe in capital punishment, but it was more like the idea of being strapped in the electric chair even though you didn't commit the crime. That song, and others on the record, were about not being able to escape a situation. Lars and I are both control freaks, and the idea of not being able to get out of a bad situation is a fear we both have.

GW You've indicated in the past that your family was quite religious. The lyrics to "Creeping Death," which deal with the Biblical stories of Egypt and the plagues, strike me as the product of someone who grew up in a religious household.

HETFIELD Or had just watched the movie *The Ten Commandments*. [*laughs*] I recall us sitting at this guy's house one day, and the movie was on TV. When it got to the part where the first Pharaoh's son is taken and the fog rolls in, Cliff said, "Look...creeping death." And I was like, "Whoa, dude, write it down! Sheer poetry!" [*laughs*] Then I got my own copy of the movie and copied down a few lines and wrote a song.

GW So your own background had nothing to do with it?

HETFIELD [*uneasily*] Well...without getting into Sunday school and all that, obviously religion has a lot of freaky shit. I mean, to this day, the image of Jesus on the cross with all the blood and stuff is so intimidating. And there's a lot of freaky things in religion that either aren't understood or aren't meant to be. But really, the whole idea of a fog rolling in and killing a few people was a strange thing to me and made for some good subject matter in a heavy metal song in 1984.

GW How did you react when the band was attacked for the lyrics to "Fade to Black," which some thought was pro-suicide?

HETFIELD Yeah, well, you can kind of rest on the whole "Well, this is art, so fuck off," freedom-of-speech thing. But when you're up there onstage, anything you say can be taken literally, and you have to be conscious of that. There's a real sick feeling of power when you're onstage: you can start a riot or put everyone to sleep if you wanted. On the other hand, as soon as you start being "responsible" with your lyrics, you start fucking with your integrity. Writing is therapy for me, so fuck everyone else, you know?

GW After *Master of Puppets* and *...And Justice for All*, two albums that dealt primarily with death, war, religion and greed, you started writing more personal lyrics on the Black Album.

HETFIELD Around the time of the Black Album we started to become four individuals in the band. I realized that we didn't really agree on things anymore—socially, politically or whatever. We get along great, but we have different opinions on things. So when I sat down to write lyrics, I wondered what I was going to put down as "Here's Metallica, here's what we think." So instead of going outward and looking for issues to talk about, I did a U-turn and went inside of myself. That was where the universal bit came in, because most people have those feelings—fucked-up, happy, sad or whatever. They're all there to be tapped into. And that's kinda the beauty of writing from the heart—you really can't go wrong.

I can remember when I wrote the lyrics to "Enter Sandman," [*producer*] Bob Rock and Lars came to me and said, "These lyrics aren't as good as they could be." And that pissed me off so much. I was like, "Fuck you. I'm the writer here!" But when I went back, I dug harder, and I came up with some stuff that obviously worked quite a bit better. That was really the first challenge from somebody else, and it really pissed me off—but it also made me work harder. From then on, I've thought twice about everything I've written. Now I rewrite stuff over and over to get it right.

GW It's interesting that you went that long without being challenged on your lyrics.

HETFIELD Well, you know, back then, I was "the man." No one fucked with the Mighty Het. [*laughs*] That's why Lars and Bob had to gang up on me that time.

GW Do you think people take you seriously as a lyricist?

HETFIELD It's still kind of a running joke that somebody's gotta sing, so I'm doing it. When we first started out, I wanted to just play guitar, and we wanted to find another singer and be a five-piece. To us, you had to have a separate frontman to make it. All the bands did: Iron Maiden, Judas Priest, AC/DC, et cetera. But I ended up doing both. And since the singer usually writes the lyrics, I figured, Shit, I better start writing some lyrics. [*laughs*] But as time went on, I decided that I wanted to take things more seriously. In the beginning, I was afraid to have my vocal loud in the mix. I felt that it didn't matter what I sang about, and that it was a chore to go into the studio and sing. But it slowly became more and more of me, and I started to take it more seriously.

GW You took writing about personal issues even further on *Load* and *ReLoad*.

HETFIELD That's just what's coming out of me right now. That's what feels best and less clown-like for me. When you're writing honestly, you can't be the clown.

11

"I don't care how much technology
ever exists—nothing can duplicate the sheer
power and feel you get from
standing in front of
your amp and bashing
on your guitar."
—*JAMES HETFIELD*

BASH TO THE FUTURE

Metallica's James Hetfield and Kirk Hammett
demonstrate that cutting-edge technology
and the heaviest metal known to man and
God can be perfectly compatible.

BY ALAN PAUL

IFTEEN YEARS AGO, even Nostradamus, the acclaimed 16th century visionary, wouldn't have been able to predict that Metallica would end the millennium as the reigning kings of rock. When they released their debut album, *Kill 'Em All*, in 1983, the band simply seemed too heavy, too fast and too underground to ever hit the mainstream. But by the early Nineties, Metallica had succeeded beyond anyone's expectations, earning the respect of critics and the support of millions of record buyers. In doing so, the group rewrote the rules for heavy metal bands everywhere.

Not that any of this came quickly or easily. Metallica achieved their success the old-fashioned way, through years of hardcore touring and a relentless effort to evolve with the changing times.

Over the course of eight studio albums, Metallica—in particular, guitarists James Hetfield and Kirk Hammett—have shown an uncanny talent for incorporating new influences and technologies into their music without losing sight of their unique creative vision. And in the process, they've learned some invaluable lessons about how to make records.

"Sound quality meant nothing to us when we started out," says Hetfield. "It was just a matter of getting the songs on tape."

By way of example, Hetfield points to "Hit the Lights," the direct-to-cassette debut track Metallica contributed to the 1982 *Metal Massacre* compilation album. "The *Metal Massacre* version of 'Hit the Lights' was taken off a four-track Tascam recorder," he says. "It went from cassette to two-inch tape to vinyl. We didn't know anything else, so we handed the producer a cassette and said, 'Here's our songs.' For us, it was the start of a learning process.

The group used a real studio for the first time on *Kill 'Em All*. "But we still just went in and jammed," says Hetfield. "Since then, it's been a constant process of growing and learning how to function as a group and how to make records. You only get better at it as time goes by."

That's certainly been true for Metallica. In the latter years of this decade, they have continued to develop as artists, showing an uncommon ability to reinvent themselves in a genre where evolution is rarely evident. Whether exploring blues forms and audio experimentation on their recent studio albums *Load* and *ReLoad* or collaborating with the San Francisco Symphony Orchestra for two concerts this past April, Metallica makes music on their terms. We asked the uncompromising duo of Hetfield and Hammett to tell us what they make of the current state of music and what the next millennium might hold for the world of rock guitar.

GUITAR WORLD Is there any undiscovered musical territory left for guitarists to explore? Or will the future involve simply refining everything that's already been discovered?

JAMES HETFIELD You always think everything's been done, until someone comes up with new sounds that just blow you away. There's always somewhere new for it to go.

KIRK HAMMETT Right now, some kid in a basement or garage somewhere is making an insanely great sound by doing something that the rest of us just wouldn't think of. And whenever someone hits on a good idea, everyone else jumps on it, helping to refine it and produce further ideas.

Look at all the bands playing seven-string guitars and tuning down—they're just going lower and lower, to the point where they can't go much further. As a result they're playing relatively simple riffs that sound really cool. Who would have predicted that?

HETFIELD I look at my own guitar playing in much the same way. You think, I'm good enough. Then you go watch someone like Junior Brown or Brian Setzer and feel like a midget. It just depends where you want to go, because the guitar can take you anywhere, which is why it's always been so popular. And people who take it somewhere different than you always seem more exotic, and therefore, better. Maybe those guys look at us and think, Wow, I wish I could bash the hell out of my guitar like that. Or maybe not. [*laughs*]

GW Will heavy metal exist in the next millennium?

HETFIELD Absolutely. It will definitely be alive in someone's head somewhere. It might be stuck in someone's basement, or it might be hugely popular, but it will always be there. Something's probably brewing right now, because people are getting really sick of Boyzone and all this pop fluff going on right now. "Heavy" has to come back and destroy

that stuff. Those are all record-company bands put together by marketing departments, just like the Monkees were. We've been through other eras like this, and something totally different always comes around
next and sweeps that stuff away. It moves in cycles. So watch out.

HAMMETT Metal's not going anywhere as long as there are people
with frustrations and rage, and a need to let them out. It helps people
vent, and everyone periodically feels the need to do that. That's never
going to change.

GW Will rock continue to be important in people's lives?

HETFIELD Perhaps not across the board, but definitely to a certain
segment. There are music fans who live by it, and fans who just put
it on when they're stuck in traffic. The people who live by it are the
youth, and they're looking for music that moves them and allows
them to live through the music by means of the lyrics. They're looking
for a way to express their feelings. That's how rock started, and rock
will continue to be there and be important as long as there are artists
who can provide that means of expression and tap into the rebel vibes
that the music has always thrown off.

GW What do you consider to be the best guitar-related innovations
since you started playing?

HAMMETT The Whammy Pedal is one of my favorite new things.
The possibilities of what can come out of it are amazing. Everyone
has a different approach to it and does something different with it,
so it offers a unique way of expressing yourself. It's not like a wah
pedal, where you can step on it on the beat and get a sound similar
to everyone else. If you gave a Whammy Pedal to five people, you'd
get five radically different approaches.

I also think Floyd Rose tremolos are pretty incredible. You can
get all the sounds that are on the Jimi Hendrix and Van Halen albums

without going out of tune. Before I used them, I'd try to copy a Hendrix move, then spend a half-hour retuning and checking the intonation.

Amplifiers are also great these days. Two- and three-gain stage concepts are just wonderful. They're still pretty much overlooked, but they're crucial to the sound of Metallica and many other bands today.

GW What would you say are the three or four most important records ever made?

HAMMETT I'm in a heavy jazz period right now, which probably colors my choices; but the creation of bebop opened the door for improvisation across the board, not just in jazz but also in blues and later in rock. So I'd have to say the first few Charlie Parker albums were very important. Miles Davis' *Kind of Blue* also opened up an entirely different world for jazz by exploring modes and using minimal chord changes. That, in turn, came to have a big effect on rock. *Bitches Brew* is another amazing album, a feat of abstract musical forms on which Miles Davis once again opened up a whole new world, creating jazz/ rock fusion. And I think God touched John Coltrane on *Giant Steps*. The forces that were stroking him are phenomenal and inspiring on an emotional and technical level to any musician.

As for rock albums, I think Jimi Hendrix's *Are You Experienced* speaks for itself, as does *John Mayall's Bluesbreakers featuring Eric Clapton*. They set new standards and possibilities for rock guitar. Likewise, on Santana's debut album, Carlos Santana mixed Latin music and rock and blues in a way that sounds natural now but at the time was really groundbreaking. [*laughs*] I knew I couldn't limit myself to three or four albums.

HETFIELD The Sex Pistols' *Never Mind the Bollocks* stood the music world on its head and made everything simple and passionate again after all the fancy, progressive Seventies stuff, which had taken rock further and further away from its original rebellious intent. I think that all of the Zeppelin records were tremendous and important—for a bunch of reasons, but mainly because they kept unveiling new ideas and new sounds. The most important album in that regard was *Led Zeppelin III*, because they unveiled all the acoustic sounds. A lot of people thought it was horrible and would kill rock. But it actually opened up a whole new world of melodies and sounds, and the purity of just a voice and an acoustic guitar spoke for itself on that record. Soundwise, I think the Beach Boys' *Pet Sounds* was really important. The experimental vibe they had there was tremendous.

GW What kind of impact do you think the internet has had and will continue to have on music? Is it a force of good or evil?

HETFIELD It's not that simple, because it's both good and bad. One really annoying outcome of it is that people have too much information. Music clips pop up there, tidbits of information zoom around and get exaggerated, and all of a sudden everyone knows what your record is gonna sound like before it comes out—or they think they know. People end up dissing you and saying you sold out a month before the album is even released. [*laughs*] And it's the same with everything: people are reading scripts before they see a movie and they know how every special effect was created. It's not just behind-the-scenes; it's behind-the-scenes of the behind-the-scenes. Whatever happened to just seeing a movie and going, "Wow, that's cool!" Why do you have to know how everything is done? It takes the mystery out of it, and that's a big loss. I used to buy records because I liked the cover art or thought the song titles sounded cool. The whole idea of "mystique" is just gone.

On the other hand, the internet makes it extremely easy to get your demo out to people. That's created a real flood of music, which can be overwhelming, but at the same time it's great that it's so accessible. When we started out, the only way to be heard was by circulating cassettes and getting into fanzines, and having a little buzz spread slowly by word of mouth. That forced bands to pay some dues and put in the time playing and getting better, but it was also hit-and-miss, and a lot of great bands fell apart before they were ever really heard. You had to get signed to be heard outside of that little circle. A record deal was the Holy Grail.

"The possibilities of the internet are tremendous. **The record companies are shaking in their little booties right now** because they won't have as much control over new artists."
—*HAMMETT*

Record companies can be bypassed now, so they have to learn how to harness that medium, which they are desperately trying to do right now. Basically, record labels are just banks, and they're becoming less important to musicians because it's easier to record and distribute your own music. There are some important things that they do for us in terms of marketing and support, but getting signed to a label is not as crucial as it once was.

HAMMETT The possibilities of the internet are tremendous. I think it has the potential to change music altogether. Some guy recording in his garage in Casper, Wyoming, can create something so totally different and original that no one's ever heard anything like it. He can then walk over to his computer and upload it to the internet as an MP3 sound file, where someone might recognize it for what it is, and then the word will spread. And just like that, a new genre of music will exist without any official product ever having been released. That's how rap and hip-hop became popular, except they grew through the streets, and the internet is the same thing to the millionth power in terms of its ability to reach masses of people quickly. Something like that could happen in weeks or months instead of years.

Once the technology is established and in use, the potential for a lot of new things to be created and distributed is just amazing. The record companies are shaking in their little booties right now because they won't have as much control over new artists. They are claiming that you won't get paid if your music doesn't go through them, but that's just their side of the story. The truth is, a lot of bands will be able to be heard on a worldwide basis, and they'll be able to charge for it. And the price of CDs will go down because the record companies won't be adding their usual overhead to it. The entire hierarchy is going to change.

GW Major changes in recording technology have also occurred during your career, specifically with the rise of ADAT and Pro Tools. Have these been good or bad for the health of music? Don't musicians gain something by being forced to figure out how to get a good sound?

HETFIELD Well, sure, but that hasn't really changed. You still hear sounds in your head and have to figure out how to make them. You don't just push a button and call it up. I think the ADAT revolution is definitely a good thing. I'm on the new Primus album just because I went over to Les Claypool's place and jammed for a while. He called me up and said, "Come over and record something. We need some heavies." So I went over to his studio, which is in his guesthouse. The group have done their last two or three records in there, and they get some amazing sounds, in part because they're being pressured like they would be in a studio, where the clock is ticking and the meter's running. A home studio is relaxed—there's none of the nervousness or annoyance of hangers-on showing up and bugging you. Plus, you can go in at any time and record whatever you want whenever inspiration strikes you. That's another very liberating and, I guess, democratic progression.

The Pro Tools thing is a little too much for me, however. It's too far removed from the organic way of making music, and I think you can tell when bands rely on it too much. I mean, we just played a show with Ministry. I love their records, but they didn't cut it live and I think it's because their music does not spring from a bunch of guys making music together. That's almost a foreign concept to a lot of bands now, which is pretty sad.

HAMMETT Right. Pro Tools can be very helpful at times, and we have used it to tweak a note that's slightly out, or to fix an overlapping beat. But our prevailing attitude in the studio is to just play the song. There are bands who play a verse and a chorus and then construct a song of three verses and four choruses, and I think that can be a problem, because if the music sounds too perfect, it loses something. I'd rather sound perfect by playing a guitar for four hours than by playing a riff once and tweaking it on a computer.

Sweat also produces results, and nothing beats the good old-fashioned method of sitting in a room and playing together and grabbing a vibe. At least for our type of music, nothing beats just sitting down and chugging it out.

GW Does that make you think live performance will continue to be important to rock bands?

HAMMETT Well, it has to be important, because it's the only valid way of establishing a grassroots following. You can't sit around and wait for radio to discover you, and I think a lot of bands realize that. And the demand for live performances will always be there because people like to see the real thing. To see people making music together is great and very inspiring, especially for a young musician.

HETFIELD That's true. I sure hope live performance will continue to be important to young musicians, because I think that's a lot of what's wrong with some of the new bands—they don't want to play live and pay their dues. You've got to pay some dues to have any validity, to find out what's really in you, how good you can be and in what direction you want to head. I feel that Metallica has had a long, steady climb, so that when we finally had success, not only did we sort of deserve it but we knew who we were.

That's really important for the overall health of music. In my mind there's a huge question about what artists are going to be holding up rock music in the years to come. You've got to have a live following. You've got to go out and tour and meet these people and show them who you are and what you do. Just selling CDs doesn't mean shit, and we need more bands ready and willing to pound the road. Because one thing will never change: I don't care how much technology ever exists—nothing can duplicate the sheer power and feel you get from standing in front of your amp and bashing on your guitar and feeling it come reverberating back onto you. Nothing beats a guitar through an amp.

REPRINTED FROM *GUITAR WORLD*, MARCH 2005

[12]

"I started thinking, If Brian Robertson
from Thin Lizzy played on this song,
what would he play?"
—KIRK HAMMETT

METAL REFLECTORS

Kirk Hammett and James Hetfield look back on
some of Metallica's brightest moments.

BY DAN EPSTEIN

METALLICA'S 1983 DEBUT, the explosive *Kill 'Em All*, taught a grateful world a lesson in unbridled thrashing fury. Since then, their sound has passed through numerous stages, but the guttural intensity that was the hallmark of the young Metallica remains the essence of the band today.

Over the past 27 years, Hammett and James Hetfield have established themselves as metal's quintessential guitar alliance. In the following retrospective, Kirk and James take a walk down Metallica memory lane and critique some of the key songs in the band's harsh, noble history.

"SEEK AND DESTROY"

KILL 'EM ALL (1983)

JAMES HETFIELD The idea for "Seek" came from a Diamond Head song called "Dead Reckoning." I used to work in a sticker factory in L.A., and I wrote that riff in my truck outside work. This was our first experience in a real studio. I used a white Flying V, which was the only guitar I had back then. I still have the guitar in storage. The song is based around a one-note riff that was up a little higher. Though most of my riffs are in E, that one worked off an A.

KIRK HAMMETT When I was doing that guitar solo, I was using James' Marshall amp. That was *the* Marshall—it had been hot-rodded by some L.A. guy, the same guy who hot-rodded Eddie Van Halen's Marshalls—and when it came time to do my guitar leads, I just plugged into that. I had maybe four or five days to do all my leads. I remember thinking, There's 10 or 12 songs on this album, so that means two a day. I had to throw down a solo, not think much about it, and move on.

I had my trusty old Ibanez Tubescreamer, my trusty wah pedal and my black Gibson Flying V that I used on the first four albums. It was either a '74 or a '78, I'm not sure. I didn't have much really worked out; I knew how I wanted to open the initial part of the solo after the break, so I just went for it two or three times. And then the producer said, "That's fine! We'll use it!" There were no frills, no contemplation, no overintellectualizing—we weren't going over the finer points. On a couple of notes in that solo, I bend the notes out of pitch. For 18 years, every time I've heard that guitar solo, those sour notes come back to haunt me! [*laughs*] I remember on that tour, whenever it came time to do that guitar solo, I was always like, Okay, I'm gonna play this *so* much better than the way I recorded it!

I had been taking lessons from Joe Satriani for, like, six months prior to joining the band, so his influence was pretty heavy in my mind and in my playing. He passed down so much information to me, I was still processing a lot of it. When it came time to do the solo, I was thinking, I hope Joe likes this. I hope this isn't something he'll just pick apart, like he has in the past.

"THE FOUR HORSEMEN"
KILL 'EM ALL (1983)

HETFIELD Dave [*Mustaine, Metallica's original guitarist*] brought that song over from one of his other bands. Back then it was called "The Mechanix." After he left Metallica, we kind of fixed the song up. The lyrics he used were pretty silly.

HAMMETT Prior to recording that song, we put in a slow middle section that wasn't there when I first joined the band, and it needed a slow, melodic solo. I remember going through the song with everyone, and when I got to that part, I played something really melodic. Lars looked up at me and said, "Yeah, yeah!" He's a big lead guitar fan. One of his biggest influences is Ritchie Blackmore. For that song I put down one lead, then added one on a different track. I wasn't sure which one to use. I listened to both tracks at once, to see if one would stand out. But playing both tracks simultaneously sounded great, and we decided to keep it like that on the record. Some of the notes harmonized with each other, and I remember Cliff [*Burton, bassist*] going, "Wow, that's stylin'—it sounds like Tony Iommi!"

"CREEPING DEATH"
RIDE THE LIGHTNING (1984)

HETFIELD We demoed "Ride the Lightning" and one other song in the studio before we recorded the album, so there's actually a demo somewhere of those three songs with different lyrics. When we did the crunchy "Die by my hand" breakdown part in the middle, I sat in the control room after we did all the gang vocals, and everyone was just going nuts! That was our first real big, chanting, gang-vocal thing. There was almost some production value to it. That whole album was a big step for us. By then I had the Gibson Explorer. I grew to love that shape better than the V.

HAMMETT When we first began playing that song in the garage, I noticed that the lead guitar part also incorporated the chorus. I thought that was a good opportunity to play something a bit wild and dynamic. The first figure in that song pretty much came off the top of my head. I was still using the black Flying V and the Boss distortion pedal through Marshall amps, with a TC Electronics EQ. For that song, Flemming [*Rasmussen, engineer*] suggested that I double-track the solo, which made it sound a bit thicker and fuller. We did that solo, after which we had to do this small fill at the end, a four-bar break with four accents afterward. The plan was to fill the break up and play something over the four accents. When I studied with Joe Satriani, I did this chordal exercise, a diminished chord with four notes. I just played that over these four accents, and it worked out real nice.

"FADE TO BLACK"
RIDE THE LIGHTNING (1984)

HETFIELD That song was a big step for us. It was pretty much our first ballad, so it was challenging and we knew it would freak people out. Bands like Exodus and Slayer don't do ballads, but they've stuck themselves in that position which is something we never wanted to do; limiting yourself to please your audience is bullshit.

Recording that song, I learned how frustrating acoustic guitar can be. You could hear every squeak, so I had to be careful. I wrote the song at a friend's house in New Jersey. I was pretty depressed at the time because our gear had just been stolen, and we had been thrown out of our manager's house for breaking shit and drinking his liquor cabinet dry. It's a suicide song, and we got a lot of flack for it, [as if] kids were killing themselves because of the song. But we also got hundreds and hundreds of letters from kids telling us how they related to the song and that it made them feel better.

HAMMETT I was still using the black Flying V, but on "Fade to Black" I used the neck pickup on my guitar to get that warm sound. I played through a wah-wah pedal all the way in the "up" position. We doubled the first solo, but it was harder to double the second solo in the middle because it was slow and there was a lot of space in it. Later I realized that I harmonized it in a weird way—in minor thirds, major thirds and fifths. For the extended solo at the end, I wasn't sure what to play. We had been in Denmark for five or six months, and I was getting really homesick. We were also having problems with our management. Since it was a somber song, and we were all bummed out anyway, I thought of very depressing things while I did the solo, and it really helped. I played some arpeggios over the G-A-B progression, but we didn't double track that solo. When that was finished, I went back and did the clean guitar parts behind the verse. James played an arpeggiated figure while I arpeggiated three-note chords. We ended up getting a very Dire Straits–type sound.

"THE CALL OF KTULU"
RIDE THE LIGHTNING (1984)

HAMMETT Again, we were using Marshalls; I tracked the whole album with Marshall amps and my Gibson Flying V. For that song,

I knew that I wanted to come up with something really melodic at the beginning of the solo. At that point in the song, there's just a lot of riffing, a lot of heavy dynamics. I was thinking, Wouldn't it be nice if we had something somewhat melodic to lead into it? Hence that little melody I played. I can remember thinking, Fuckin' hell, man, these guys want me to play an awful-long fucking guitar solo! It was our first instrumental, and it was an incredibly long guitar solo. It was, like, How can I keep this solo going without making it sound like I'm just playing a bunch of notes? So I thought that I would break it up into sections rather than play one long spew of notes. I used a modal approach, and there are also arpeggios that I play in the solo. They're actually "broken arpeggios," a term that I got from Yngwie Malmsteen. At that time,

"The idea for 'Welcome Home (Sanitarium)' came from the movie *One Flew Over the Cuckoo's Nest*."
—*HETFIELD*

1984, Yngwie was big in the guitar world; he influenced me in that he was using all these different scales and different arpeggios, and really got me thinking about that kind of sound. I was also thinking chromatically: there's that one part at the top of the next cycle where I play a chromatic lick that goes all the way down the high E string with the wah pedal.

I actually wrote out the entire solo on pieces of paper, using my own notes and my own pet names for the individual licks. I would say that 80 percent of it was composed beforehand and 20 percent of it was improvised. When we revisited that song with the symphony on *S&M*, it was a lot of fun. It felt like I was visiting my guitar technique from, like, 15 years ago or something. I just don't play like that now— I'm a lot bluesier—so it was pretty trippy.

"WELCOME HOME (SANITARIUM)"
MASTER OF PUPPETS (1986)

HETFIELD The idea for that song came from the movie *One Flew Over the Cuckoo's Nest*. "Fade to Black" worked well, and we wanted to have another slow, clean, picking type of song, this time with a chorus. I had trouble singing that chorus. It's really high, and when I went to sing it in the studio, I remember Flemming looking at me like, "You're kidding." I said "Shit, I don't know if I can do this!" So I ended up singing it lower than I intended, but we put a higher harmony on it and it worked pretty well. The riff for that song was lifted from some other band, who shall remain anonymous.

HAMMETT The beginning of the first solo is an arpeggiated ninth chord figure, where I basically mirror what James is playing. The second guitar figure had some harmonies. I used a wah-wah pedal on the third solo, which was pretty straight ahead. The fourth solo comes out of harmonized guitars; the very last lick was based on something really cool I saw Cliff play on guitar in the hotel one night that I knew would work in that spot.

"MASTER OF PUPPETS"
MASTER OF PUPPETS (1986)

HETFIELD I think we wanted to write another song like "Creeping Death," with open chords carried by the vocals and a real catchy chorus. On *Master of Puppets* we started getting into the longer, more orchestrated songs. It was more of a challenge to write a long song that didn't seem long. The riff for that song was pretty messy—constantly moving. It works good live. People love to scream "Master!" a couple of times.

HAMMETT I used my Jackson Randy Rhoads V for this solo. When you listen to the solo, there's this weird sound right after the mellow part where it sounds like I'm hitting a super-high note in the midst of my phrasing, like I'm fretting the string against the pickup. Well, what happened was, I had accidentally pulled the string off the fretboard! You know how you take an E string, you pull it down toward the floor away from the neck? I accidentally pulled down on the string, and it fretted out on the side of the fretboard. We heard it back, and I was like, 'That's brilliant! We've gotta keep that!' Of course, I've never been able to reproduce that since; it was like a magic moment that was captured on tape. That was one of my most favorite things about that guitar solo. I thought I had screwed the solo up by accidentally pulling on the string, but once I heard it back, I thought it sounded great. That was definitely a keeper!

For the next solo we used backward guitar parts. To get them I played a bunch of guitar parts that were in the same key as the song and laid them down on quarter-inch tape. Then we flipped the tape over and edited it, so we had two or three minutes of backward guitar. We put it in the last verse of the song.

A lot of people think I actually came into my own sound on that song. That had everything to do with buying Mesa/Boogie Mark II-C heads. Boogie made those heads for a short time in the mid-Eighties and only made a limited amount of them. They moved on after that, and they haven't really been able to recapture that sound since—I don't know if they ever tried or not. But there's something about Boogie Mark II-C heads that were really unique and very individual in their gain stages and overall sound. Most of *Master of Puppets* was tracked with Boogie heads and Marshall heads combined, and I used my Gibson Flying V and my Jackson. By that time, I also had my black Fernandes Stratocaster.

THE $5.98 E.P.: GARAGE DAYS RE-REVISITED (1987)

HETFIELD Putting out an EP of all cover tunes was absolutely unheard of, which we thought was really cool. We didn't do too many arrangements, except to some of the Budgie tunes, where we eliminated some lame singing parts. For some of the songs we tuned down to D to make them a little heavier. The guitar sound is really awful, but it was the first thing we put out where the bass could be heard, so Jason [*Newsted, bassist*] was happy.

HAMMETT That was recorded when I first started using ESP guitars with EMG pickups. All the lead guitar parts on that EP flowed really quickly. I did them in two nights. All of the leads were mine. The fact that the original versions of "Helpless" and "The Wait" don't even have solos in them was a bit of luck—no one would have anything to compare them to, and it kept any preconceived ideas out of my head. We did that EP for the fans, just for fun, and Elektra loved it and released it.

"...AND JUSTICE FOR ALL"
...AND JUSTICE FOR ALL (1988)

HETFIELD That song is pretty long, like all the songs on that album. We wanted to write shorter material, but it never happened. We were into packing songs with riffs. The whole riff is very percussive; it goes right along with the drums. The singing on that song is a lot lower than usual.

HAMMETT I worked out an opening lick for the solo but it wasn't really happening, so I plugged in the wah-wah pedal, which I always do when all else fails. As soon as I plugged in, we were done. A lot of people give me shit about how I hide behind the wah pedal, but something about it brings out a lot of aggression. It just tailors the sound to match the mood and emotion I'm trying to convey. It's purely an aesthetic thing and not a crutch or anything like that. The riff where I utilize the open string hammer-ons developed from a Gary Moore lick that I'd been studying. I figured it would sound really good combined with the heavy E-chord progression.

"ONE"
...AND JUSTICE FOR ALL (1988)

HETFIELD I had been fiddling around with that A-G modulation for a long time. The idea for the opening came from a Venom song called "Buried Alive." The kick drum machine-gun part near the end wasn't written with the war lyrics in mind, it just came out that way. We started that album with Mike Clink as producer. He didn't work out too well, so we got Flemming to come over and save our asses.

HAMMETT I lost a *lot* of sleep over that set of guitar solos! [*laughs*] The main guitar solo at the end, with the right-hand, Eddie Van Halen–type tapping came almost immediately. That guitar solo was just a breeze; what was going on with the rhythm section in that part of the song was just very, very exciting for me to solo over. The first solo was a little bit more worked out. I heard James playing some really melodic stuff over the intro, just doodling around, and I thought, That's pretty cool, I'm gonna use part of that. So I have to give credit to James for subliminally pushing me in that melodic direction. I think the first two licks at the top of the first solo are his, and the rest of the solo just sort of fell into place. That little chord comp thing in that first solo came from a major-chord exercise that I do all the time. I thought it would sound really good in the solo if I just staccato-picked it and resolved it right there. I thought the solo needed something to perk people's ears up!

The middle guitar solo in that song, I must have recorded and re-recorded it about 15 million times. I wanted a middle ground between the really melodic solo at the beginning and the fiery solo at the end. I wanted that to sit very confidently within the song, but it sounded very unconfident and I was never happy with it.

Finally, it came down to the wire: we were mixing the album while simultaneously touring on the Monsters of Rock tour. One night, I flew from Philadelphia to New York City, and while everyone else was on their way to Washington, D.C., I went to the Hit Factory and rerecorded the solo again. I brought my guitar, I had one of my main amps sent to the studio, and I redid the solo there and finally nailed it. I was very, very happy about that! The next day, we played a show in Washington, D.C. It got panned by the critics, because we'd all only had about three hours of sleep and were exhausted. But I got a good solo the night before, so it was worth it!

We wanted a clean guitar sound for "One." I think at that point I was using the ESP neck-through-body KH-1 guitar, with the skulls on the fingerboard. I'd gotten that guitar in '88 and used it pretty prominently in the studio. I used an ADA preamp and an ADA MP-1—it was a programmable digital amp that had tubes in it, with a separate rack-mounted Aphex parametric EQ. I remember blending that thing with the Boogies for lead sounds and clean sounds. The clean sound on "One" was done almost exclusively with the ADA MP-1.

"ENTER SANDMAN"
METALLICA (1991)

HAMMETT Again, I was playing my ESP with a wah pedal, and this time I used a bunch of different amps. We were combining Boogies and modified Marshalls; I also think we had a clean old Fender in there, and maybe even an old Vox amp, and they were all blended together to get that tone. I can remember getting that lead guitar sound together very quickly, very spontaneously. When it came time to start thinking about that guitar solo, I just thought, Well, this is a great guitar song, and it's in the spirit of all my favorite guitar bands, like Thin Lizzy and UFO, but kind of modernized. So I kept thinking, Michael Schenker, Michael Schenker... But then I started thinking, If Brian Robertson from Thin Lizzy played on this song, what would *he* play? With that mindset, I started playing what I thought Brian Robertson would play on a song like that, and the entire fucking guitar solo wrote itself!

You know how the guitar solo plays out, and then there's a lead guitar break that leads into a breakdown? I think the time has come to tell where I actually got that lick. It's from "Magic Man" by Heart, but I didn't get it from Heart's version; I got it from a cut off Ice-T's *Power* album, where he used it as a sample. I was listening to *Power* a lot while we were recording *Metallica*, so I kept on hearing that lick. I thought, I have to snake this! I did change it around a little bit, though.

"DON'T TREAD ON ME"
METALLICA (1991)

HETFIELD A lot of the songs on this album are more simple and concentrated. They tell the same story as our other shit but don't take as long. There aren't a hundred riffs to latch on to—just two or three stock, really good riffs in each song.

I used my ESPs and tons of other guitars: a 12-string electric, a Telecaster, a Gretsch White Falcon, a sitar and other things. I also used a B-Bender, a bar installed in the guitar that twists the B string up a full step. It's used a lot in country music. But "Don't Tread" is just real heavy guitar—there's really nothing else to it.

HAMMETT I used a Bradshaw [*preamp*] because the mids were clean and the low end sounded real percussive, and I put it through a VHT power amp. The harmonic distortion also sounded nice and dirty. For the highs we used two Marshalls. We combined all the sounds and put it all through Marshall cabinets with 30-watt speakers and blended all the room mikes. My sound is a lot thicker and punchier than before, and I think it's better than ever. For the majority of the leads on this album I used a third ESP guitar. I also used my 1989 black Gibson Les Paul Custom. For the clean sound, I used a '61 stock white Strat and a Fender blackface Deluxe. I also used a '53 Gibson ES-295 style, and an ESP Les Paul Junior with EMG pickups.

I used the '89 black Gibson Les Paul Custom and a wah-wah pedal on "Don't Tread on Me." At one point I had to play these ascending lead fills, and it just wasn't happening at all. So I wound up playing harmonics instead of lead guitar fills, and it worked really well.

"THE GOD THAT FAILED"
METALLICA (1991)

HETFIELD That's a very nice song. Slow, heavy and ugly. There are a lot of single-note riffs and more open-chord shit on this album. A lot of the rhythms I came up with were a little too complicated—half-step changes and other weirdo shit that Kirk had trouble soloing over. So we simplified some things. All the harmony guitar stuff on this album is incorporated in the rhythm tracks. I played rhythm all the way through, then I overdubbed harmony guitar things. There are harmony solos and harmony guitar in the rhythms, but they're very distinct from each other. We found that layering a guitar six times doesn't make it heavy.

HAMMETT I had this whole thing worked out, but it didn't fit because the lead was too bluesy for the song, which is characterized by real heavy riffing and chording. So producer Bob Rock and I worked out a melody, to which I suggested that we add a harmony part, but Bob said it would only pretty it up. So we ended up playing the melody an octave higher, and it sounded great. We basically mapped out the whole solo, picking the best parts from about 15 solos I'd worked out. It's one of my favorite solos on the album.

One thing I did on this album that I hadn't done before was play guitar fills. I filled up holes—like when James stops during the vocal, I put in a little stab or, as Bob calls it, a "sting." My solos on this album are a little offbeat. Though a lot of guitar players start the solo on the down-beat—the first beat of the measure—I come in on the upbeat of the third measure of a bar, like on "Enter Sandman" and "Don't Tread on Me."

"HERO OF THE DAY"
LOAD (1996)

HAMMETT The first time James heard my solo on "Hero of the Day," he didn't like it. He said, "It sounds like bad Brian Robertson!" [*laughs*] I was, like, 'What do you mean?' And then, after much 'debating' back and forth, we kind of agreed that it wasn't so much the solo that was the problem but the lack of anything going on underneath it. So he went and put something down underneath it that made it sound, well, a little better to his ears, I guess. It was one of those things where one musician hears one thing one way and another musician hears it completely different.

For the *Load* album, I was experimenting so much with tone that I had to keep journals on what equipment I was using. For "Hero of the

> "I was experimenting so much with tone that I had to keep journals on what equipment I was using."
> —*HAMMETT*

Day" I know I used a 1958 Les Paul Standard with a Matchless Chieftain, some Boogie amps and a Vox amp—again, they're all blended. I was listening to a lot of David Bowie at the time, particularly the sounds on *Low*, and I was really interested in playing guitar *parts* to see if I could shape the character of the song by playing parts instead of solos. And to a certain degree that's what I was trying to do during "Hero of the Day." It's a guitar solo in the classic sense, but it's a part of the song as well. I was very into the idea of creating soundscapes and crafting textures. I was tired of playing ripping, shredding solos; I wasn't into proving myself like I was around, say, ...*And Justice for All*. It's great to be able to have that in your back pocket and use it when necessary. But for the most part, taste, tone and atmosphere are my main concerns.

I'll tell you a funny story, though. In '94, a guy came up to me and said, "How come you stopped doing double stops? You used to play a lot of double stops, and then you stopped doing it. I miss it." And when we were recording *Load*, all of a sudden I remembered him saying that. I thought, Yeah, you know, he's right! So in that song "Better Than You," which ended up on *ReLoad*, I just crammed both solos with all sorts of double stops. And that was totally for that guy."

"FUEL"
RELOAD (1997)

HAMMETT That track was actually recorded at the same time we were doing all the *Load* stuff. It was one of the first tracks [*from that session*] that I actually played a guitar solo on. That guitar solo was played through a couple of old Marshalls, some Vox amps and the Chieftain, and I used a 1963 Sea Foam Green Strat. I can remember thinking, God, this guitar has such a killer sound to it! It wasn't like all my other guitars, which had active humbuckers and everything.

It sounded fat, present and full, and I was blown away by how big it sounded, even though I was going through single-coil pickups, stuff that wasn't active. That was a real treat for me, because it really felt like I was going in a new direction, tone-wise and equipment-wise. And that all kind of blossomed throughout *Load* and *ReLoad*. Bob Rock definitely had a big role in that, because he's a total equipmenthead, and he really got me thinking about vintage gear.

"NO LEAF CLOVER"
S&M (1999)

HAMMETT That song came together only about a week before we actually played with the symphony. And that week leading up to the actual dates was so hectic. We had to do so much footwork that I really didn't have as much time as I would have liked to spend on that solo. So I thought, Hell, I'll just go for it and improvise! And what you hear on that track is just me improvising, and playing off the top of my head on my ESP "Mummy" guitar. I mainly used my live rig, which consists of Boogies and Marshalls and Boogie cabinets. My rack-mounted wah is in there, and that's about it, other than maybe just a touch of delay.

There's a modulation toward the end of the solo, and I kind of wanted to outline that modulation a little bit. That's why I shift keys for the four or eight bars at the end. The solo on "No Leaf Clover" is actually comped from the best licks from both nights and made into one solo. In retrospect, I would have loved to have had more time to structure it and put it together. But we were on a deadline, blah blah blah, and we really didn't want to rerecord anything—we wanted it to all be recorded with the symphony. So we just kind of went for it."

[13]

It really felt like **there was no future for Metallica."**
—*KIRK HAMMETT*

MONSTER'S BRAWL

Fights! Camera! Action! What started as a simple
documentary about Metallica nearly became an
account of the group's destruction. *Guitar World*
goes behind the scenes of Metallica's critically
acclaimed new movie, *Some Kind of Monster*, for a
scorching blow-by-blow report.

BY RICHARD BIENSTOCK

ⓂMETALLICA

197

THERE'S A SCENE THAT occurs roughly an hour into *Metallica: Some Kind of Monster*, the band's intense new documentary. Drummer Lars Ulrich, pacing the floor at the band's HQ studios in San Rafael, California, looks across the room at singer and guitarist James Hetfield, fresh out of rehab and still struggling to readjust to the outside world, and offers him a comforting welcome home. "When I was running this morning," says Ulrich, "I was thinking about seeing you today, and the word *fuck* just [*came*] up so much."

Hetfield, who had been nestled away in a rehabilitation center for more than six months battling alcohol addiction and various other life-afflicting demons, sits silently as Ulrich begins repeating the word, mantralike. "Fuck," he snarls at the man with whom, more than 20 years ago, he cofounded what is arguably the most successful heavy metal band in history. "Fuck!" Finally, Ulrich moves in close, until the two are practically nose to nose, and screams one last time: *"Fuck!"*

It's a particularly intense and ugly moment in a film that has no shortage of either. *Some Kind of Monster* tracks Metallica from the sudden departure of bassist Jason Newsted in January 2001 to the completion of their eighth studio album, *St. Anger*, more than two years later. Throughout the two-hour-and-twenty-minute film, which will be theatrically released in summer 2004, the actions of Metallica's core members— Hetfield, Ulrich and guitarist Kirk Hammett— are sometimes petty, sometimes reprehensible and occasionally downright embarrassing. And that's exactly what makes the documentary such a riveting piece of work. Equally impressive is the fact that Metallica, who have been practicing rigorous damage control on their image for nearly a decade, wholeheartedly endorsed being shown in such a revealing and often negative light.

"There's still part of me that fears this film will come out and **people will actually go to see it.**"
—*HETFIELD*

"Our attitude from the beginning was 'warts and all,' " says Hammett. "We said to [*filmmakers*] Joe Berlinger and Bruce Sinofsky, 'Show us good, show us bad. Just show us.' And you know, sometimes we look like assholes and sometimes we look like spoiled rock stars— but we also look like human beings. I think presenting the full picture offers more insight into who we are as people."

"There's still a little part of me that fears this film will come out and people will actually go to see it," says Hetfield. "But then there's another part of me that thinks, Hell yeah, people are going to see your struggles, they're going to see your high points and your low points and they're going to get to know you better. And that's exciting."

By now it's common knowledge that Metallica went through a rough period prior to *St. Anger*'s release in June 2003. The media coverage that accompanied the album's release often—and rightly—characterized the band's previous few years as a perpetual downhill slide that began when Ulrich crusaded against Napster and subsequently alienated the band's core fan base, continued when Newsted jumped ship after 15 years of service and bottomed out when Hetfield entered rehab for "alcoholism and other undisclosed addictions."

What was given short shrift, however, was how hard the band's members fought—as a unit and against one another—to survive each new tragedy that befell them. Their efforts included hiring a $40,000-per-week "performance enhancement coach" named Phil Towle (a move that in the film Newsted dismisses as "really fucking lame and weak") and overhauling their infamously rigid working conditions to allow each band member equal say in the songwriting process. And as the film demonstrates, Metallica struggled not only to move forward but also to confront head-on the issues that had hindered them in the past. This is no more evident than when Ulrich sits down for a one-on-one, long-overdue meeting with former Metallica and Megadeth guitarist Dave Mustaine, who was brutally fired by Ulrich and Hetfield in 1983.

"This is not a movie about the making of *St. Anger*," says Hetfield. "It's not about the music. This is a movie about the *people* in Metallica and the relationships that they share with one another and with the other individuals in their lives. The music is secondary to the whole picture."

"Hopefully," Hammett adds, "by showing what we went through, the film can give some direction to other people that are experiencing some of the same things, whether they're in a band or not. I think that we explored options that a lot of other bands wouldn't have even considered. And yeah, I know Metallica have an image as this big, indestructible entity and that a lot of the things you see in the film, like us sitting in therapy, may be viewed as signs of weakness. But I gotta tell you, we've always been known for just laying our balls on the line and saying, 'Fuck it.' "

Over the years, that tendency has resulted in the band receiving more than its fair share of criticism, and many of the scenes in *Some Kind of Monster* will only inspire more such attacks. Anyone who has written off the band's post–Black Album career as nothing more than an across-the-board sell-out bid for mainstream acceptance will only have those feelings justified watching as James, Kirk and Lars begrudgingly record an ass-kissing promo spot for a radio station contest. Similarly, Ulrich's post-Napster image as an arrogant, money-grubbing aristocrat is blown up to almost parodic proportions in one scene filmed at a swanky New York City auction house. As his pricey art collection is sold off for millions of dollars, the drummer sits in a private room, gleefully sipping champagne while an orchestral version of "Master of Puppets" plays softly in the background.

But moments like these are the film's essence. *Some Kind of Monster* isn't meant to be a glossed-over, *Behind the Music*–style infomercial disguised as an exposé; it's more akin to pulling back the curtain on the Wizard of Oz and finding that, far from being all powerful, he's quite human, vulnerable and flawed. And that's where Metallica, for all the "warts" exposed, are most successful. Love them or hate them, you cannot deny that their career has had more than its fair share of trailblazing, uncompromising and inspiring moments. *Some Kind of Monster* is simply yet another triumph.

And the whole thing almost never happened.

WHEN METALLICA FIRST MET with Joe Berlinger and Bruce Sinofsky to discuss working on a project together, the band was, in fact, interested in a promotional tool that could help sell a new album. The group had struck up a relationship with Berlinger and Sinofsky while the pair were working on *Paradise Lost: The Child Murders at Robin Hood Hills*, their 1996 documentary about the trial of three heavy metal–loving teens convicted of murdering three young boys in West Memphis, Arkansas, in 1993. In their film, Berlinger and Sinofsky argued that the boys' affinity for wearing black clothing and listening to metal music was ludicrously inadequate proof of their guilt. They had hoped to license several Metallica songs to use in the project, and had faxed what they thought would be a futile request to Q-Prime, the band's management.

"At the time Metallica had never granted the rights to let their music be used in a movie," says Berlinger, "and we figured that even if they did, they would charge a lot of money for it. But we got a call back an hour after we sent the fax and it was like, 'Sure, what songs do you want?' Apparently, the band were big fans of our first film, [*1992's*] *Brother's Keeper*, and they liked what we were doing with *Paradise Lost*. And to top it off, they gave us the music for free, no strings attached. And that's how our friendship began."

Despite numerous discussions over the ensuing years about a full-blown collaboration between the two parties, the closest they came to working together was when Berlinger and Sinofsky produced a Metallica episode of the short-lived VH-1 series *FanClub*. "Other than that, the whole idea died," says Berlinger, "because we hit an impasse. Bruce and I wanted to do a film that took a very personal look at the band, while management had more of a clips-driven, historical thing in mind that they could run on an HBO or an MTV to help them sell product."

It wasn't until the end of 2000 that the idea was revived. At the time, Berlinger was reeling from the critical lambasting of his big-budget Hollywood directorial debut, *Book of Shadows: Blair Witch 2*, a movie whose failure he blames on the studio "basically putting my cut into a blender and puking it out into the theater." Berlinger thought it might be therapeutic to resurrect the Metallica project. To his surprise, management responded to his new inquiry with the news that Jason Newsted had just quit the band, Metallica were about to begin recording a new album with producer Bob Rock handling bass duties, and all the members, including Rock, were taking part in group therapy sessions. How would he and Bruce like to film the whole thing?

"It was like being dropped into Vietnam during the war without any preparation, and all of a sudden you're right there in the thick of it," says Sinofsky. "And there were no handlers or managers saying, 'You can't do this' or 'You can't do that.' It was just like, *boom!*—a month or two after the first phone call we're filming a therapy session. I remember Joe and I looking at each other during those first few shoots and thinking, We don't know where this is going, but it's going to be unbelievable."

"A film like this you can't really plan out," says Hetfield, "like, 'Hey, let's start rolling tape, and maybe something traumatic will happen soon!' But things did start happening, and Joe and Bruce were there to capture these pivotal points in our personal history, which we then had an opportunity to share with the world. And if those things hadn't happened, we would have merely had an 'in the studio' type of film that would have been used as promo material."

As filming dragged on for more than a year—a time period that included a long and dormant stretch during which Hetfield was away in rehab—the project came dangerously close to being turned into a promotional vehicle. Elektra, Metallica's record label, was anxious to reap benefits from its investment and pressured the filmmakers to wrap production. The label hoped to fashion a block of "reality TV"–like segments from the raw footage and air them concurrent with the release of *St. Anger*. But Metallica, believing the film had the potential to tell a much bigger story, opted to buy out their label's 50 percent share of ownership (at a price of $2 million) and allow Berlinger and Sinofsky to complete the project as they saw fit.

Although Hetfield, Hammett and Ulrich are now the sole owners of *Some Kind of Monster*, it's apparent from the final cut, culled from more than 1,600 hours of footage, that they didn't place any constraints on the directors. Berlinger, for one, believes that is precisely what makes the film so impressive. "If these guys didn't have complete control over the movie and weren't paying for it out of their own pockets, it wouldn't be as remarkable. The things you see wouldn't have the same impact if Bruce and I were just two independent newsmen who dug up some dirt on the band and shoved it into a movie. Metallica could have told us to take out anything that they decided they didn't want the public to see, but they treated us as if we had final cut. There's absolutely nothing that they kept out of the film."

"I'll tell you," adds Sinofsky, "if I were Lars, James or Kirk, there are certainly moments in the film that *I* would've demanded to have deleted. That art auction scene? Lars was pressured to take it out by many people in the band's inner circle—from wives to managers to lawyers—who all told him that it's no good for his image. And to Lars' credit, he was like, 'Fuck it! This is who I am.' And you have to have respect for that."

FOR ALL THE TALK ABOUT Metallica and the filmmakers not wanting *Some Kind of Monster* to function merely as a promotional tool for *St. Anger,* in some indirect ways it does just that. Upon the album's release last year, many fans put off by its minimalist song structures and raw production accused the band of lacking the passion and commitment that had always characterized its best work. But it's evident in the film that, for Metallica, creating *St. Anger* was more than a labor of love—it was literally hard labor, requiring more dedication and determination than perhaps any record in their career.

Throughout the film, the band members—in particular Ulrich and Hetfield—battle over riffs, drum beats and lyrics, and break out of their strictly defined musical roles to help one another with their parts. (The lyrical hook "My lifestyle determines my death style" from "Frantic" is revealed to be not a Hetfield-composed rehab mantra but rather one of Hammett's Zen-like axioms.) Furthermore, the first section of the film is littered with recorded attempts at songs that didn't make the final cut of *St. Anger.* One tune, in which Hetfield repeatedly sings the word "temptation," is built on a slow, doomy riff and a tom-heavy drumbeat that sounds like nothing else in Metallica's recorded history.

"If we didn't go through those songs we wouldn't have made it to the ones on *St. Anger,*" says Hetfield. "They were like stepping stones.

There's some pretty diverse music in there, just a mix of a lot of different things we tried. We wanted to explore every possibility."

Some Kind of Monster also lends greater insight to the album's lyrics, which typically have been interpreted in terms of Hetfield's rehab experience. Many of the songs do address issues the singer dealt with during that period, but it's not the only subject confronted. The film reveals that "Shoot Me Again"—with its refrain, "All the shots I take/I spit back at you"—is about Ulrich's fight with Napster and the criticism he endured over it, while the opening line of "Sweet Amber"—"Wash your back so you won't stab mine"—is a phrase uttered by a disgusted Hetfield after he's informed that Metallica's refusal to record the radio promo spot could result in their being blacklisted by the large conglomerate that owns the station.

And then there's "My World," a song that could almost be a group catharsis. In one of the documentary's final scenes, the band is shown jamming the song, whose lyrics deal with regaining control over one's own life. *St. Anger* has been completed, new bassist Robert Trujillo has joined the fold, and Metallica, once again functioning as a complete unit, are preparing to go out on tour. It's at this point the group decides to give Towle his walking papers. The therapist has become too close to the group; he's even attempted to contribute lyrics to *St. Anger*'s songs. (Earlier in the film Hetfield remarks that Towle is "under the impression that he's, like, in the band.") The band meets with Towle and effectively ends their working relationship. Afterward, Hetfield is shown singing the opening line from "My World," "Who's in charge of my head today?"

"When I came out of rehab I was like raw hamburger," Hetfield explains. "Anyone could have shaped me into anything they wanted.

So when Phil started doing things like handing me lyrics to sing, it was like, 'Well, this *feels* weird, but am I being too rigid? Maybe I need to accept things and open up more.' I didn't know where the boundaries were. At some point it became obvious to me that I was totally confused as to where the business part ended and the friendship began. And it seemed to fluctuate whenever Phil needed it to."

"But," adds Hammett, "he also really helped us accomplish what we needed to get done. It was just that, toward the end, things started to go a little haywire."

"I believe that the band is together today because of Phil," says Berlinger. "And yeah, he got a little too close, but I don't think that was a bad thing, because for Metallica the final stage of the program was to push him away. Part of the growth process is that children need to flee the coop."

For all its focus on therapy, *Some Kind of Monster* contains one session fans will be most anxious to see: it's when Ulrich sits down with Dave Mustaine to talk at length, and possibly for the first time, about Mustaine's firing from the band in 1983 due to his hard-partying ways, and about the effect the dismissal has had on his life. As Ulrich sits in near silence, his eyes watery and often averted toward the floor, Mustaine describes the pain of having to watch, as he describes it, "everything that you guys do...turn to gold, and everything I do fucking backfire." It's an intensely revealing scene that lends a human touch to a story that, over the years, has become a part of heavy metal folklore. While he places the blame for his ouster squarely on his own shoulders, Mustaine takes Ulrich to task for the hostile way in which it was handled, noting that, unlike Hetfield, he was never given the option of attending rehab, and how, over the years, neither Lars nor James had made a genuine attempt at reconciliation.

Mustaine has since made it known that he is unhappy with his portrayal in the film, and although he declined to comment for this story, this past January he posted a cryptic message on Megadeth's official web site in which he wrote the movie off as "Some kind of bullshit" and stated, "I noticed how much footage they used [*of the meeting*] and to whom it benefited, too." Berlinger and Sinofsky, for their part, are confused by Mustaine's reaction.

"My experience with Dave was that he was a real gentleman," says Berlinger. "I know that when he showed up he was a little surprised to see the cameras, but I explained to him what we were doing, and he signed a release form giving us permission to use the footage. The whole meeting between him and Lars lasted about two or three hours, and we turned off the cameras three times, at his request, when things got a little too emotional. We tried to be very respectful of his feelings."

"Here's a case where the truth shouldn't hurt," says Sinofsky. "The Metallica and Megadeth fans who see this film will probably get a better understanding of Dave Mustaine than they have in 20 years."

"The guys in the band are aware that Dave isn't happy with that scene," says Hammett. "But he said what he wanted to say, and nobody put any words in his mouth. Dave had free reign to present himself however he wanted to. And if he feels now that he didn't present himself in the proper way, is that really our fault?"

FOR ALL THE FOCUS ON relationships in the film—be it Dave Mustaine coming face to face with his former band mate or a bunch of heavy metal he-men sitting around discussing their feelings with a middle-aged, bespectacled therapist—one relationship in particular is clearly at the center of *Some Kind of Monster*: that of James Hetfield and Lars Ulrich, the two men who were there when Metallica began, and who will be there, for better or worse, when they end. What the movie makes apparent is that the band's demise was actually a lot closer than perhaps anyone realized. Berlinger admits that there was a point during the filming where he and Sinofsky "were pretty sure that we were making a documentary about the disintegration of a band." After one particularly nasty scene in which Hetfield and Ulrich argue over the latter's choice of drumbeat for a song, Hetfield storms out of the room and doesn't return—for months. It was during this time that he checked himself into rehab and cut off all contact with the rest of the band.

"It really felt like there was no future for Metallica," says Hammett. "I had to start thinking about backup plans, like, Maybe I should make a solo album, or maybe I should start raising horses."

"In all honesty I wasn't sure if I *was* going to come back," admits Hetfield. "And that was needed in order for me to come back in a healthy way. I had to ask myself, 'Who am I?' I have to walk around with the idea that people have pumped into my head that, 'Hey, you're the dude in Metallica. That is your worth. If you're just a person on your own you're not worth as much.' Which is total crap. I had to realize that I could live without the band in order to live with it again. And I think that was scary for Lars, because I came back to the band as a different person, and it's tough when someone else's changes in their life begin to affect your own. Especially when the two people involved are both egocentric control freaks!"

Hetfield delivers that last statement with a laugh, but it's clear that there is also some truth to his words. Which raises an interesting question: Is friction between great egos a necessary ingredient for all successful creative partnerships? Were the notorious clashes

"**I have so much respect for all of the guys**, not only for what they were willing to go through to save their band, but also for having the guts to let us film it."

—*FILMMAKER BRUCE SINOFSKY*

between legendary duos like John Lennon and Paul McCartney, Mick Jagger and Keith Richards and Steven Tyler and Joe Perry in part responsible for their creating some of rock and roll's most enduring music? According to Hetfield, the answer is not quite so clear.

"That friction does help in some instances, but I don't think it's absolutely necessary. Because you see some musical writing teams that get along great, and even some that are husband and wife, and you think, My God, how can they work together *and* live together? But they do, because different people work off of different energies. In the case of Lars and I, we worked a lot of the time off of negative energy and also off of perfectionism. We were the kings of pushing each other further—like, Hey, to make this better I'm gonna drill you! As a result, there was this atmosphere of, Okay, I know he's gonna say this, so I've gotta get my armor on, and then retaliate this way—just a lot of fear and defensiveness. But we've come to understand that it doesn't have to be that way. We each have really clear and excellent visions of what music is for us, and we can realize those visions without making the other guy suffer."

Hammett, for his part, states in the film that he forever tries "to be an example of being egoless to the other guys." Throughout *Some Kind of Monster* he's constantly playing the role of mediator between Hetfield and Ulrich, attempting to keep things running smoothly so that the band can continue working. "Egos create gridlock," reasons

Hammett. "If I started in as well, there would just be *three* egos battling instead of two."

"In the film, Kirk is always the guy saying, 'Come on, let's not beat on each other,' " says Sinofsky, "while Lars is constantly pushing to that next level. James is clearly the one with the most problems, and his story is so inspirational because he's willing and able to overcome those problems. I have so much respect for all of the guys, not only for what they were willing to go through to save their band but also for having the guts to let us film it, and now to show it to the world."

Fans may view *Some Kind of Monster* as a heroic epic, cautionary tale or merely voyeuristic, reality TV–type fodder. What's certain is that, for the members of Metallica, at least, the film contains many important lessons that they will continue to learn from in the years to come.

"Cliff Burnstein [*Metallica's manager*] was asked what he thought the value of *Some Kind of Monster* will be," says Berlinger, "and he said, 'Forget about the publicity, or if it's going to make money or help to sell some albums—forget about all of that. The most significant thing the film is going to do for these guys is that when things start to fall apart two, three, 10 years from now, I'm going to sit them all down and make them watch it again. It will be a very important vehicle to remind them of what their relationships can be about.' "

"That's a really cool way to look at it," says Hammett. "This film can be a lesson for the future that was created in the past—sort of a reminder to ourselves, from ourselves. I mean, really, how great a gift is that?"

[14]

"We've never been known to
take the easy way out."
—*KIRK HAMMETT*

THE PHOENIX

Kirk Hammett tells why Metallica burned their bridges with *St. Anger* and explains how they rose from the ashes to create *Death Magnetic*.

BY BRAD TOLINSKI

KIRK HAMMETT IS WIRED *and* tired. In approximately one hour, Metallica will hit the stage of the Wiltern Theater in Los Angeles to raise money for the Silverlake Conservatory of Music, a nonprofit music school for low-income students. While Hammett is psyched to be playing for this great cause, there is no denying that, at the moment, he's draggin' ass.

"I tried to sleep in this morning, but I couldn't because I'm on baby time," he explains. "I have a one-and-a-half-year-old, and my wife's giving birth to another baby in about six weeks. I've been getting up at 6:30 in the morning, so this is already getting late for me.

"I'll have to reset my rock and roll clock if I'm going to have any chance of making it through the next tour," he adds, laughing.

Hitting the reset button has become a theme for Hammett and his band over the past year. After spending much of the decade redefining their sound, Metallica have gone full circle and returned to the crunching, thrash-metal style that established them as the world's greatest hard rock band in the Eighties. While it's tempting to attribute this dramatic about-face to their superstar producer Rick Rubin, Kirk explains that the band did much of the heavy lifting on their new album, *Death Magnetic*, themselves.

"Rick was important because he planted the creative seeds, but he left the lion's share of the execution to us," Hammett explains. "It was a great relationship, because he gave us guidance but left our core intact. For example, if there were anything he thought was substandard, or just wrong for us, he would just tell us to write something else; he wouldn't try to tell us how. There was a lot of mutual respect."

When asked why, after 20-plus years in the business, Metallica didn't just produce the record themselves, Hammett laughs and shakes his head. "We need an outsider, or else a lot of creative decisions would become stalemates and we'd never get anything done," he says, referring to band's notoriously turbulent relationship. "We need a tiebreaker. Maybe if there were a fifth person in the band it could work, but at this point we're not about to get a keyboard player."

One thing the band could apparently agree on was to give Hammett plenty of room to rip. Considering that he was all but forbidden to play solos on the group's previous studio effort, *St. Anger*, it's both a shock and a relief to hear him cut loose on *Death Magnetic*. As frontman James Hetfield explains in the accompanying interview, putting one of the greatest soloists in rock history on a short leash probably wasn't a good idea. To Metallica's credit, they've more than made up for the error by allowing Hammett to play fast, loud and long throughout *Death Magnetic*. In fact, one could argue that Kirk practically owns the album.

The mellow surfer-dude yin to James's tough-guy yang, Hammett takes this vindication in stride. In the following interview, he talks with modest pride about his new lease on *Death* and how goddamn good it feels to be "face melters" once again.

GUITAR WORLD How would you describe *Death Magnetic*?

KIRK HAMMETT I would say it sits somewhere in between ...*And Justice for All* and the Black Album. It has an aggressive, technical side, like *Justice*, but there's also a lot of melody, like the Black Album. We wrote the album with every intention of it being just a kick in the face, and I think we pulled it off. We've been working on it for long enough—close the three years. At one point we had 24 songs, and we had to tear it down to 14, and it has even fewer now, but I think it's everything that we wanted to hear.

GW Was there a lot of discussion about how the band wanted the album to sound, or did the sound unfold naturally?

HAMMETT I remember we had a meeting with Rick Rubin back in 2005, and we had already written some music, and we played it for him. We talked about what he wanted to hear from Metallica and what his ideal Metallica album would be like. He also planted the seed in our heads that it would be okay for us to reference our past. So during the entire creative process we allowed ourselves just to be ourselves.

It was actually very exciting to be able to look back at the formulas that worked for us in the past and gather new inspiration from them. We gave ourselves permission to take the best aspects of our past and combine them with the best aspects of what we are now to create something totally different.

GW You should be allowed to plagiarize yourself. Everybody else has stolen from Metallica.

HAMMETT Yeah. [*laughs*] Well, we spent a long time trying to distance ourselves from our early music to prove to ourselves that we're more than just that. And that's pretty much what the Nineties were. We were just exploring our own potential creatively and figuring out what we were capable of and what we could get away with. We've passed that. And now we just wanna go out there and be the world's heaviest band again.

GW Are you conscious of how much your sound has permeated metal?

HAMMETT Yeah, it's interesting. I'll put on satellite radio and hear something and think, Hey, we did that in 1987! Who is this band? It's flattering, and it's fun for us. I don't think we see that as a negative thing at all. I only say that because you can imagine how an artist might think they're being ripped off. I see it as a tribute.

GW It might be beyond that. They probably grew up listening to Metallica, and to them, that's just the way metal should be played.

HAMMETT Yeah, our sound is part of the lexicon. The *metal* lexicon!

GW How would you say you've changed as a guitarist from, say, ...*And Justice for All*?

HAMMETT Well, I went through a whole blues period in the Nineties and that had some influence on *Load* and *ReLoad*. Then I started listening to a lot of jazz—stuff like Kenny Burrell, Tal Farlow, Grant Green and Wes Montgomery—guys who were just monsters on the guitar. It was a great education, because I discovered where all of my rock heroes got a lot of their licks. Jeff Beck, Clapton, Hendrix, Stevie Ray Vaughan and Jimmy Page all took ideas from those players and turned them into the vocabulary of their generation.

I drew it all in, and it changed my style totally. However, a couple years ago I started feeling like I was going too deep. I'm back to being primarily a metal guitarist, but some of the blues and jazz ideas have changed me in important ways. My improvisation skills have really improved—I flow a lot better; I'm putting a lot more faith in my abilities to be spontaneous—whereas in the past I would compose my solos. Ninety percent of the time my solos on past albums were composed, where now, I would say, it's maybe 40 percent.

I've been pushing myself to the limit in the studio—right to the very edge of the abyss. And I took my playing into areas I've never been before. I'm currently relearning the songs for our upcoming tour, and I'm scratching my head going, "What did I do there?" I can't remember what I did, and I can't figure it out. I might need the transcribers at *Guitar World* to help me! [*laughs*]

GW One of your thrash metal contemporaries, Alex Skolnick of Testament, has recorded a couple of straight-up jazz albums as the Alex Skolnick Trio. Have you heard them?

HAMMETT Love them. I love his work. What Alex is doing by putting heavy metal songs in a jazz context is completely refreshing. His take on [*the Kiss classic*] "Detroit Rock City" [*from 2002's* Goodbye to Romance: Standards for a New Generation] blew me away; that song has never sounded better to me. I have a friend who is a total jazz nut, and he says that Alex's three CDs are some of the most important things to happen in the jazz world in a long time. When you think about it, all the old jazz standards were the pop music of the time. And we're *still* playing those jazz standards.

He's updated the notion of what a standard is, and it's opened up all the current music to interpretation. The idea of playing Kiss or the Scorpions in the style of Dave Brubeck is great and quite radical. There are tons of people at Julliard who are playing [*Thelonious Monk's jazz standard*] "Straight No Chaser" for probably the 50 millionth time, so it's about time somebody tried something new.

GW I was playing your ESP Mummy guitar, and I noticed that your action is quite high. You definitely have some fight in your guitar.

HAMMETT The fight brings out more emotion. If a guitar is too easy for me to play, it makes me too laid back. I like to battle with my guitar. My pick attack is hard, and when the action's too low and you have a hard attack, things just start buzzing all over the place.

GW When I was talking to James, I thought it was interesting that he returned not only to his classic sound but also to the instrument and amplifier that he used on a lot of Metallica's Eighties recordings. Your sound, however, is quite different from those albums—it's bigger and has less bite. Many of the solos have a really bold, singing quality.

HAMMETT I've added more midrange to my overall sound. I can still appreciate my original scooped sound, but I *need* to feel the ground shake when I hit a chord. It hasn't been any radical change in gear as much as it's been a change in EQ. For *Death Magnetic* I used what I always use, which is my standard touring rack, which is filled with some Boogie stuff and a Marshall that I've had forever. I also used the new Randall amp that I helped design, and Greg Fidelman, our engineer, turned James and me onto Ampeg heads. Ampeg made incredible guitar heads in the early Nineties and then stopped. And I don't know why. The one we used had a nice clean, warm sound, and it blended well with the other amps that were in the studio.

I'm a total vintage freak and would have liked to use more of my collectible amps, but we got the sound that worked for the sonic context, and I really didn't want to make it more complicated. The same goes for guitars. I used a few vintage guitars here and there. I think I used a '58 Paul and a '59 Tele on some clean stuff, but overall, almost everything is done on my ESP Mummy and the Caution guitar, which is the original Scully guitar—the very first ESP guitar, from 1987.

GW When you do your solos, do you get input from the other guys?

HAMMETT Lars helps me, because when I'm doing solos, it's hard for me to be objective. I'm a soloing machine! On one song, I played over 100 solos. And when I play more than five or six solos, it's hard for me to be objective. So Lars helps me out, and he'll often tell me what's working and what isn't.

It's good, because what he's really doing is pushing me and inspiring me to go into directions that I wouldn't think of because I'm too in the moment. For the most part, I'm very much a team player. I like to hear what other people have to say, provided they're qualified.

GW What do you think that you learned from *St. Anger*?

HAMMETT I was shocked by how much people missed guitar solos and my playing on *St. Anger*. I just thought it would be water off their backs, and it wouldn't be that big of a difference. On tour, however, at least five people would ask me every single day why there weren't guitar solos on the album and if there were going to be guitar solos on the next album. To tell you the truth, I had no idea that people considered that aspect, or that ingredient, to be such a large part of our overall sound. I always saw myself more as icing on the cake. But goddamn it, man, those people really like that icing!

I've learned that there's a signature Metallica sound, and if we stray too far from that, our fans get impatient, or they just don't understand, or they miss the point. And I'm not saying that's a good thing or a bad thing; it's just something we have to contend with.

GW It's a sound they can't get from anyone else.

HAMMETT There is some truth there. In the Nineties, we probably spenttoomuchtimedeconstructingthatsound.Wediditintentionally, but we oversimplified. Along with that oversimplification came whatever was influencing us at the moment. But I agree with you.

You can't really get Metallica anywhere else but from us, and I think people got the impression that we were just holding back.

GW I can understand how any band could get bored with doing one thing. You have to be able to go someplace else creatively.

HAMMETT I wouldn't say we were bored as much as we were restless. We had put out four or five albums using, basically, the same sort of approach, and we were wondering what else we could do and what else we were capable of. We very consciously tried to stay away from certain elements of our sound—like heavy chugging on the E string. There's none of that on *Load*, because we felt we had exhausted it.

GW Were you afraid of becoming a caricature of yourself?

HAMMETT There are bands out there that put out the same album every time and just change the lyrics. We all know who those bands are, and we were very careful to not let that happen to us. In retrospect, we might have overreacted. But now we're ready to embrace our roots again, and we're having fun. These songs are really fun to play, and at the end of the day, that's the most important thing.

GW And who knows, if you hadn't taken those turns, people might have been bored with the band by now.

HAMMETT We wouldn't be as well regarded because we would have diluted our sound with a bunch of regurgitated crap. We've never been known to take the easy way out. [*laughs*] Never. It's just the way we are. It's the way we think.

GW It's interesting that you would be surprised that people would miss your soloing. You were, after all, the first person inducted by our readers into the *Guitar World* Hall of Fame. That was over Jimi Hendrix and Jimmy Page.

HAMMETT It's crazy. Guitar playing is both extremely easy for me and extremely difficult for me at the same time. Today, someone told me that they played guitar, but they "just couldn't get that soloing thing down." And I just said, "Bro, I've been playing for almost 30 years, and the guitar is still a mystery to me. I'm still searching and finding little things here and there."

It feels like an unraveling process. I'm unraveling the guitar, and I want to find the core of it, but it's so multi-layered that I'm not even close.

GW I think people maybe identify with your sound because of the struggle to some degree.

HAMMETT I don't have a clear answer to that question. I'm too close to it. One thing I've noticed over the years is that young players—I mean 10- and 12-year-olds—really like my guitar style. There's something in my guitar style that they totally can latch onto and learn quickly, and then go from there to your Yngwie Malmsteens or your Steve Vais or whatever. On the flipside, the more mature musicians hear my stuff and go, "Eh, whatever."

GW I think one of the hallmarks of your solos is that they are memorable, which is more difficult than just playing fast.

HAMMETT That's always been my thing. I love Michael Schenker because he plays the hookiest solos. I've always been attracted to players who are not necessarily melodic but very hooky. Ritchie Blackmore has a very hooky style, and he's not very melodic at all. A lot of times, the stuff he plays comes out of left field, but it's catchy, and there's an integrity to it that just kind of pulls at you.

From the very beginning, I've always put taste, phrasing, tone, melody and hookiness before speed and pure technicality. I've always played for the song, and I've always played to entertain people. And I've never purposely played anything to alienate people.

When you play a great lick that you haven't played before, it's amazing, because it feels like it's been handed down to you from the heavens. It flows through your fingers, onto the strings, to the pickups and out the amp, and suddenly you hear this great thing. You recognize it as the entire creative process. And sometimes that happens so quickly and so unexpectedly. It's as if there's a big crack in the ground and this big hairy paw hands you this heavy guitar riff. There are no preconceptions, no premeditations. I'm sure it happens to most dedicated musicians. It may not happen as often to the casual strummer, but if your heart is into it, it happens.

GW How do you account for this?

HAMMETT I'm way into the metaphysics of the subconscious and multi-dimensional thinking. I know that vibrations connect all of these things. And if you really want to get technical, I buy into the string theory of physics. The basic principle is that everything in the universe is made of these vibrating strings. It's nice to think that the cosmos is essentially a huge guitar and inspiration comes when I'm tuned into it.

GW Speaking of connections, it's well documented that Metallica went through some tough times regarding your relationship to one another during the making of *St. Anger*. Do you guys feel reconnected?

HAMMETT Totally. The communication is as good as it's ever been. Before *St. Anger*, and at certain times while we were making the album, our camaraderie fragmented to almost nothing. You can almost say that *St. Anger* was the struggle to get that camaraderie back, but now we have it again, and it's evident on all levels—on a performance level, on a personal level and on a creative level.

GW Sometimes you have to strip everything down to basics in order to build it back up again.

HAMMETT Or maybe burn it down. Metallica is like the phoenix rising from the ashes. We set everything on fire, and this is what has risen from it, *St. Anger* being the fire and *Death Magnetic* being the phoenix.

[15]

"There's nothing cooler than when people use one of my ideas to discover themselves."
—*JAMES HETFIELD*

V WILL ROCK U

James Hetfield returns to his roots,
picks up his original Flying V and vows once
again to kill 'em all.

BY BRAD TOLINSKI

WITH HIS BLACK WORK SHIRT, black jeans and big, black motorcycle boots, James Hetfield looks a little like a garage mechanic working the graveyard shift at a funeral home. His thoughts, like his outfit, are dark.

"The theme of our new album is that we're all gonna die sometime," he says with a cruel little chuckle. "Just like the poles of a magnet, some people are drawn to death and others are repulsed by it, but we all have to deal with it. Lyrically, it started as a bit of a tribute to [*Alice in Chains singer*] Layne Staley and all those who've martyred themselves in the name of rock and roll. But it grew and evolved from there."

Given the morbid nature of Metallica's ninth studio album, *Death Magnetic*, it is ironic that the recording represents something of a musical resurrection. While the 10-song recording does not slavishly imitate the group's late-Eighties triumphs like *Master of Puppets* or ... *And Justice for All* as rumored, it is not afraid to hark back to those glory days. Jammed with adventurous song structures, devilishly complex instrumental breaks, whiplash tempos and numerous guitar solos, *Death Magnetic* is the aggressive, old-school thrash epic longtime Metallica fans have been dying for. It is, in Hetfield's words, "more alive and has more lift" than anything the band has done in a long time.

THE HET IS MANY THINGS, but he's no pussy. He's the Han Solo of metal—one of those rare dudes that radiates an imperturbable, unflappable "cool." But over the past few years, even Metallica's singer and master rhythm guitarist has wrestled with his share of uncertainty.

"Yeah," Hetfield says, "the road gets cloudy. Life gets cloudy. The whole ban on guitar solos on our last album, was kind of a..."

Falling short of calling it a "mistake," it is clear that James has some misgivings about his band's previous studio effort, *St. Anger*. Featuring repetitious, grungy drop-C riffs and a surprising absence of shredding from the band's virtuoso lead guitarist, Kirk Hammett, the controversial 2003 release was Metallica's least successful studio outing.

"I wasn't a big fan of not having any solos on the album," Hetfield says. "Being a singer, there are very few songs I listen to just for the solos, but the solo *is* the voice for a little while. And not having that element on *St. Anger* was somewhat—I don't want to say 'boring'— but it made the album pretty one-dimensional. Either the singing was on or the riff was on. Or that *snare* sound was on," he says laughing, referring to the distinctive tuning of drummer Lars Ulrich's kit, which became the signature sound of the album.

At the same time, the frontman defends the validity and sound of the work, which he feels directly reflected his state of mind following his much-reported stint in rehab. "We tore Metallica down to a bare-bones skeleton, and it was not unlike what I went through in my personal life. During that period I was breaking down and rebuilding. *St. Anger* is exactly what it had to be and needed to be. With our new album, we're back into our earlier mode, where the songs are more of a ride. It's a lot more fluid."

Helping the band get back on track are superstar producer Rick Rubin (noted for his productions for Johnny Cash, Red Hot Chili Peppers, Slipknot and Slayer, among numerous others) and bassist Robert Trujillo, who took over bass duties for the group in 2003 (longtime bassist Jason Newsted quit Metallica in early 2001 to pursue other projects). The result, Hetfield explains, is a work of new "power, excitement and clarity."

As for his fabled rhythm playing, it's never been harder, faster or more precise. Warming up to the topic, James, who is often said to have the best right hand in metal, says, "I'd much rather talk about guitar playing. I hate it when people ask me about my lyrics. I always feel like telling them to just go and read them," he says with a laugh.

So with that, we begin our conversation that encompasses life, death and James' "eternal quest" to get the world's greatest guitar sound.

GUITAR WORLD How would you describe this record?
JAMES HETFIELD I guess I would say that it's a look backward—taking the essence of our earlier style and playing it with our current skills. It's impossible to completely regain your innocence or virginity. When we recorded our first albums, we had no regard for authority or for the way things were supposed to be. We'd walk into a studio

and we'd play what we knew and that was that. Some of the engineers would complain and say things like, "You can't hear the vocal" or "You can't hear the guitar...what's that sound?" And we'd say, "That's us! Record it, please." [*laughs*] We tried to capture that attitude again. It's one of the reasons we chose Rick Rubin to produce the album. He's good at capturing the essence of the artists he works with.

GW Rick is great at taking classic artists like Johnny Cash and Neil Diamond and helping them recapture what made them great in the first place.

HETFIELD Yeah, presenting them again and giving them another chance to speak. Especially Johnny Cash. Johnny was totally screwed by his record company and kind of disappeared. It's like, "Come on, Johnny Cash *is* America. This has to rise to the top again, somehow. Gotta fly the flag!"

GW The new album references the past, but it has its own character.

HETFIELD I'd like to think every one of the albums has its own unique and distinct sound. Some might be harder to listen to. Listening to *St. Anger* is somewhat of a chore for me. [*laughs*] It's cool because it's raw and in your face, but it has just one dimension. You know, "This is anger, and here it is."

GW How important is the guitar sound to achieving that character?

HETFIELD Very important. I'm on this eternal quest to get the best guitar sound in the world, but my vision of what is "the best" changes every time I go into the studio. Sometimes my goal is to make my guitar jump out, and sometimes I want it to lay back. It all depends on what we're trying to achieve with the album. But getting the right sound is essential. I want to feel what I'm playing. When I finally arrive at that sound, the songs get written and played.

GW So how did this album begin?

HETFIELD It began by reviewing lots of music we had written on the *St. Anger* tour. We usually play a little bit before each show just to loosen up. Invariably, someone will have a riff and we'll start recording and jamming. The beginning of this record was sitting down and listening to all of those sessions.

What was interesting is that the music would be very different depending on who got to the warm-up room first. Different pairings would create completely different ideas and grooves.

GW So the writing usually starts with an instrumental riff?

HETFIELD A guitar or drum riff always starts the song. That's the seed the songs rise from.

GW Each song on the new album features multiple riffs and as many as three solo sections. Did you ever worry about going over the top?

HETFIELD Well, we usually fall victim to ourselves in that respect. We always think there's not enough or there's got to be more, and most of the songs on this album are pretty long. However, we're not too concerned. We're pretty sure radio, be it satellite or whatever, will play them.

The one thing I struggle with these days is quality control. In the early days we only had to write between eight and 10 songs per record, so if a riff wasn't good we just threw it away. But that started to change when we were writing *Load* and *ReLoad*. If a riff wasn't working, instead of throwing it out we'd explore it and try to take it as far as we could to see if there was anything there. We'd end up recording 20-something songs, which was especially challenging because I had to write lyrics for all of them.

On *St. Anger*, the process was even longer; we went through two writing cycles. On this one, there were 16 *full* CDs of ideas with 30 to 40 ID markers on them. We'd name each riff. Here's the "Fargo" riff. Here's "Casper." Here's whatever.

GW Where would the names of the riffs come from?

HETFIELD It would get pretty abstract. For example we called one "Jim Bag" because the riff reminded me of a punching bag, but it also had a [*guitarist*] Jim Martin–Faith No More feel. So you shove these words together and you name the riff. And you'd *remember* what riff it is.

GW On the first few records, Metallica were inventing a new form of metal that evolved into what we now call "thrash." It was a very internal process. Then in the Nineties, you allowed more outside influences to affect your look and sound. *Death Magnetic* seems like a return to your original impulses.

HETFIELD Maybe. You'll probably get a different answer from each person in the band. Lyrically, I write what I feel. It's as simple as that. I'm not looking around saying, "Hey, this type of lyric is more popular these days."

> "It's not hard for me to play fast. It's just not. And I love that."
> —*HETFIELD*

But there is no question that we pay attention to the outside world when the bar has been raised sonically. One of the reasons we wanted Rick Rubin to work with us is because we liked the sound of his production on the Slipknot and System of a Down albums. Rick and our engineer, Greg Fidelman, brought our sound to a new level. There's power, there's excitement. It feels alive, but you can hear everything. I really believe that we've always been our hardest critics. Our attitude has always been, It better be good, or else we're not gonna put it out. But there have been times when we probably felt less like that.

GW I know you're a singer, but your rhythm guitar playing had a huge impact on a couple of generations of guitar players. How do you think your guitar playing has changed since, say, ...*And Justice for All*?

HETFIELD I haven't really thought about it. I would say I'm probably a little more precise. It's a little more important to me that the riff is clear. Back then I would just layer parts four times and make it wide. Now I'm more concerned about how sounds work. I'm a little more willing to put up with a sound that's not completely great on its own but fits well within a song.

GW You're considered to be one of fastest and most precise rhythm players in rock history.

HETFIELD [*laughs*] It's not hard for me to play fast. It's just not. And I love that. It might take a little while to warm up to certain songs, but the fast down picking—the really fast double picking in the riffs, especially when I pick up the beat—is just fun.

GW Are your guitars set up a certain way to make it easier for you?

HETFIELD I never really pay much attention to that aspect of it. Most of my guitars have been instruments that look cool. I'm not picky. I never think, Oh, this neck isn't made of ebony or These strings don't feel correct. It doesn't matter too much. Now, though, I'm paying a little more attention to what strings I'm using because they help me stay in tune. But I just like playing fast riffs. It's as simple as that. In fact, it comes so easy to me that maybe there was a time, like while we were writing the Black Album or *Load*, that I needed a different kind of challenge. But now it just feels good to go to that place.

A lot of it has to do with playing my old guitars again. I'm actually using the white V and the old Explorers that I played on the first few albums. I'm also plugging into the Mesa/Boogie Mark II C+ that we used on all the early albums.

GW What made you crack open your old guitar cases and plug in your old amps?

HETFIELD When we begin recording, we always start by trying out lots of new amps and guitars. I've often asked myself, Why do we do this? The answer is usually, Because I want to and I can. [*laughs*]

I always think I can make my sound better. So you get every amp company in the world coming in with their latest product, including prototypes of things that haven't even been built yet, and at first it's like going to guitar heaven. But then I start plugging everything in, and by the time I whittle it down, I'm back with my Eighties Mesa/Boogie "crunch berries."

GW But what got you back into using your white V?

HETFIELD That amp with that guitar is magic. No other explanation. It's not the beefiest or fattest sound, but the mids just come alive.

GW How many tracks did you use for rhythm guitars?

HETFIELD We'd have three or four amps going at the same time. We'd just morph between the tracks to see what sound felt best for the song. We used an Ampeg for some things, and I'm still using my Mesa/Boogie TriAxis preamp, but the C+ usually ended up taking over the left side [*of the stereo spectrum*], which is my side.

GW It's not surprising that you still gravitate toward your early gear. Those are the instruments that you really know. There is no way something new and unexplored is going to compete with that kind of relationship. When was the last time you got a new piece of gear and said, "I'm gonna spend a week and just work with it to find out what it can do"? You spent years with your V and your Boogie.

HETFIELD That's really true. And those early circumstances were powerful, too. I can remember when we first discovered Mesa/Boogie, back in the Eighties. We heard about this amp company right in

Pomona, near where we live. When we first plugged in, we said, "Oh, this is awesome. This is amazing. But it's how much? Oh my God!" We couldn't afford it back then. But when we finally got our hands on those amps in '83 or '84, around the time of *Ride the Lightning*, we spent weeks tweaking and working, adding pedals, adding this and that, just like you described.

GW And the white V—it's not a Gibson V, right?

HETFIELD No, it's a Japanese knockoff. It's actually the third guitar I ever owned. My first guitar was a swap-meet thing that I paid five bucks for and painted about 12 different times. I put Eddie Van Halen stripes on and all that stuff, like every kid did. And the second guitar I had was, like, a '69 SG that some kid sold me in high school for $200. I traded it for a P.A. because I wanted to be the singer, because everyone was looking for a singer back then. And then the next guitar I bought was this V.

Somebody sold it to me as a Gibson V, and as a dumb kid I had no idea. Eventually it dawned on me: Oh, it has a bolt-on neck. It can't be. *Hmmm*, why does it say "Made in Japan" on it? [*laughs*] But I didn't care. I didn't have a care in the world. It's a white V! It's Michael Schenker, it's Scorpions. That was metal: black pants, white V, go! I couldn't care less that it was not a real Gibson.

GW It created your signature sound. I'm always fascinated with stories of people finding these basic tools and making them work to create something amazing. I think most great music comes from that. It's not about having every tool. It's about working with what you have.

HETFIELD It's the struggle. From struggles come great gifts. Even though you don't know they're gifts at the time. Later on they become that. ESP makes me amazing things—anything I want, but I still use *that* guitar. It's a shitty Elektra copy of a Gibson V from the late

Seventies, maybe, early Eighties. And yet, here I am, holding it on the cover of *Guitar World*!

GW That's because it is *your* guitar.

HETFIELD I know what you mean. Well, the thing is, it's very strange, but I'm just discovering that. Somebody recently approached me and said, "We're putting a coffee table book together. Bring some of your most signature guitars out."

It started thinking about it. I actually have my own new signature guitar made by ESP, but what do people know me from? Which instruments spawned my best riffs? So we pulled out the first Explorers ESP made for me—the "So Fucking What" guitar, the "Eet Fuck" guitar, the "More Beer" guitar—and I just started playing them. It sounds cliché, but I put on these old shoes and they just fit.

I thought, This is why I play this guitar. I'm searching so hard to have my signature stuff, and it's back there! Turn around, dude—you have it! I'm grateful to have my eyes opened.

GW It's an interesting parallel. You've done the same thing with your music. You started in a place, and then you explored all these different areas, and now you've gone full circle.

HETFIELD But you don't know until you leave. You don't see home until you're gone. That's how it feels. And it's a great feeling to come back home.

GW Your rhythm playing on this album is tight, but it's less stiff and more "groovy" than on your early records. You've almost become the Keith Richards of thrash. Are you more relaxed and less self-conscious in the studio than you were in the early days?

HETFIELD Oh, I'm still insecure. For sure! I'm always saying, "It's not tight enough." People think I'm nuts. It's something that absolutely haunts me. After we recorded "Hit the Lights," which appeared on the *Metal Massacre* compilation—the one where Metallica is spelled with two Ts [*laughs*]—this guy heard the song and told me, "Oh, the rhythms aren't very tight, are they?" Man. That was it! That started my lifelong quest. That was the Holy Grail for me—being tight. Back in the early days, we were all competitive. *Very* competitive. We'd always say, "They're faster...but they're not as *tight*." That's where we got our satisfaction.

GW If I'm not mistaken, most of the new album is in standard tuning. That's a big change from *St. Anger*, which was in drop C.

HETFIELD Yeah, it's all A-440, except two songs that are in drop D. That was one of Rick Rubin's things. That's probably the biggest thing he contributed to this album. He'd always say, "I want you to play in 440. Let's hear what it sounds like." And he found there was some tonal quality, not in just the music but in the voice, too, that he really liked. There was something in the struggle of me singing in higher keys that he felt was unique.

I wasn't very excited about it, because it was difficult for me. There might be some people whose voices don't change after 27 years, but I would think it's rare. So that was a little bit of a hurdle for me. But I was willing to go for it, and it really did work pretty well, especially in the faster songs. And playing faster in 440 is quite a bit easier.

GW Much of the current thinking is, I want to sound heavy, so I'm gonna drop my tuning. But that can also just as easily turn the music into sludge.

HETFIELD I discovered that our sound was more alive, and felt younger, because it's in A-440. It's got a lift to it. Sonically, everyone was able to find his space in the mix a little better, and we sound fuller.

None of this is to take away from playing in drop tunings. When you're sitting in your room and you drop down, and you're the only guy playing, it's amazing. I'm the bass player and the guitar player!

It's like, who needs a bass player! But when you incorporate that into a band, it'll work for a couple of songs, but a whole album filled with that can sound pretty flat.

GW Even though you've gone back to using some of the original tools, your sound has changed. Your sound is a little less brittle.

HETFIELD Obviously, in the earlier days, my sound was scooped. We made a smiley face on the EQ, and that's it. During the time of the Black Album we learned more about using the guitar's midrange—adding more mids, getting a little more what I call "bark." The "bark" is found in the low mids, where your guitar is very percussive and hopefully marries up with the drums and makes everything sound even punchier. It's an element that has become pretty important to me.

"On the Black Album we learned how to **add muscle to our sound.**"
—*HETFIELD*

GW How involved are you in the mixing or the engineering processes?

HETFIELD During the recording process, we'll all work and get the sounds we like as individuals. I'll say, "Here's the sound that makes me play well." Then, the engineer's job is to make all our sounds live together properly. Sometimes there's give and take, but *my* guitar is pretty important. [*laughs*]

GW Are you happy with the sounds?

HETFIELD I'm very happy with them. And I'm pretty surprised at how we got them, too. We went a lot drier and used a lot less gain. When I chug, you feel the compression suck on the cabinet. Add the razory top provided by the V and the C+—the combination works really well together.

In the early days I played all the rhythm guitars and Kirk played the lead. Then things changed on *Load* and *ReLoad*; Kirk did a lot of rhythms. On this album we returned to the way we originally recorded. All the rhythm parts are me.

GW What did you learn from the Black Album on?

HETFIELD On the Black Album we learned how to add muscle to our sound. On *Load* and *ReLoad*, I learned that when you write too many songs, your focus gets watery; it gets diluted. I hate that part of us. We know how to take an okay song and make it good. But the question lately has been, Do we have the discipline to dismiss an average song and say it's not on the record? Do we know when something is not good enough?

We used to have that discipline early on. And I attribute that to having blinders on—that fuckin' attitude that says, "Fuck that, it's not heavy enough to put on the album." In the Nineties we tried to embrace everything, and [*producer*] Bob Rock was good at helping us do that. Each time we did, we opened our eyes a little more, but the discipline kind of went away. We became craftsmen instead of destructors. So from *Load* and *ReLoad*, what I learned is that I can't spread it out over 40 songs. I just can't. I'd rather have eight powerful songs than 14 so-so songs.

GW That's almost been the crime of the CD. The reason why a lot of those classic rock albums kick ass so much is because there's eight tight songs, not 13 loose ones.

HETFIELD Lars and I battle constantly about that. I'd rather have eight that are going to get people *hard*, and he'll go, "Let's play 'em all." I don't want fluff. I don't want extra stuff. I don't want bonus tracks. I don't want, "You gotta give 'em more." Fuck that. I want to give them *good*. And if it's good, they're gonna want more. It's as simple as that. That frustrates me a lot. And he and I go back and forth on that.

GW You've talked a bit about Diamond Head and the music that inspired you when you were first starting out, but is there somebody that you've listened to in the past 10 years, whether it's a new or old artist, that you appreciate on a guitar-playing level?

HETFIELD [*Long pause*] There are certain guys who obviously inspired me to play guitar. I loved certain bands. Ted Nugent and Aerosmith had some riffs, but it was more the Judas Priests and the AC/DCs that got to me because the rhythm guitar was such an important part of their sound. I'd listen to somebody like Malcolm Young and think, This dude's driving the train right now. And that would be exciting. These days, there's been such an amazing resurgence in guitar talent—and not just guitar but drums, keyboards, singing... It's unbelievable.

GW Yeah, that Pro Tools guy is pretty good!

HETFIELD [*laughs*] Yeah. Mr. Tools? Yeah, he's one helluva producer! I hear what you're saying, but I think there's more to it. I think there are guys sitting in their bedrooms trying to imitate stuff that has been Pro Tooled to death, and they're playing it naturally. Pro Tools is creating new monsters. It's amazing how some of these guitar players are. It reminds me a lot of, say, when the Eighties happened and all of these amazing virtuoso guitar players like Yngwie Malmsteen were emerging, and there were plenty of bands that had amazing rhythm sections.

GW Are you talking about bands like Bullet for My Valentine and Avenged Sevenfold? Their arrangements are so big and complex that they are almost writing heavy metal symphonies.

HETFIELD Right, right. You can probably put DragonForce in there. Bands that have two unbelievable guitar players and they're playing all their parts perfectly in concert. And the drummer is keeping right up with them. There are drummers around these days that blow me away. And some of the stuff is very orchestral. It's very dramatic and epic sounding. So a lot of that stuff is pretty inspiring.

And then you get the bands that are really sideways—Meshuggah or Loincloth. They make me wonder, How in the fuck can you remember this song? How can you? It's unbelievable. With some of this stuff, it's almost too much and hard to listen to at times, but I'm just stunned. It's a pretty exciting time.

GW It's cool that you still keep up with a lot of the new bands. I like many of the bands you just mentioned, but in many cases the singers are the weakest links. You've got 'em whipped on that level.

HETFIELD Think so? Well, we're still looking for a singer. [*laughs*] If one walks in, we're still looking. I'm just filling in for now. But then you have the other side of that where you've got some bands that can really sing and you hear them all on the radio. They've got these singers that are singing, basically, this poppy melody. They're trying to sing it gruff, and they've got the heavy guitars, but it's pop. It's fuckin' pop. And it's driving me nuts. I'm so sick of it. That's why I'm really gravitating to more of the stuff on Hard Attack, the real heavy station [*on Sirius Satellite Radio*]. Even though a lot of singers are hard to take, I'd rather hear something that's alive. Something someone put some thought into.

GW The production on *Death Magnetic* sounds pretty organic.

HETFIELD I'm not saying that things were not fixed, by any means. There's a lot of that going on. But the key to that is to not lose the feel. A lot of times it's the push and pull between Lars and me that's either good or not. That's a lot of it—the magic of the feel.

GW But you don't feel any push and pull on some of the modern metal records.

HETFIELD Well, for some bands it's "robot" all the way. But you know what? I love hearing that for a little while. I like to get blown away by the fuckin' metal robot. [*Makes machine-gun drum sounds*] You know, stuff that is just hammering you.

When you're in your car rivaling some guy next to you, and he's got his rap [*makes hip-hop bass sounds*] rattling his tuner car apart, and you've got the '52 Oldsmobile and you're firing machine-gun drums at him, it's pretty cool to be able to rival that with some good sonics.

GW At the top of the interview you said you'd rather talk about the music, but your lyrics are pretty hard-hitting on *Death Magnetic*. What were you going for?

HETFIELD I really wanted to focus on the crypticness of the Metallica lyrics. I wanted them to be somewhat anonymous but powerful. If you're in that frame of mind, you'll plug into it. I'll put two powerful words together, and sometimes I won't know what they mean, but I'll apply them to my life somehow. The thing I don't like is when songwriters are blatant and they say things like, "I wrote this song about this." I like to put intense ideas together and let them morph into people's lives and souls. The hope is that it can apply to other people's fucked-up-ness. There's nothing cooler than when people use one of my ideas to discover themselves. It's their own therapy, in a way.

REPRINTED FROM *GUITAR WORLD*, APRIL 2009

[16]

lways felt that *...And Justice for All* was writ
from Metallica's heart and not their head.
t's a total masterpiece.
—*ADAM JONES*

METAL
ALCHEMY

They both started as cult heroes—Metallica's
Kirk Hammett was a man of the people, and Tool's
Adam Jones was a man of mystery. Join them as
they compare notes on how they transformed their
heavy metal into a worldwide religion.

BY BRAD ANGLE

IT'S ONLY 5 P.M. WHEN I arrive at the Forum in In-glewood, California, but the parking lot of this classic 18,000-plus arena is already crowded with metalheads of every age, shape, color and gender, all eating and drinking in anticipation of tonight's show. Above the din, a familiar metal re-frain blasts from a stereo:

> *The Horsemen are drawing nearer*
> *On leather steeds they ride*
> *They come to take your life.*

And what better soundtrack to prepare for the four bringers of tonight's metal apocalypse—Metallica's James Hetfield, Lars Ulrich, Kirk Hammett and Robert Trujillo—than their own ripping ode to

Armageddon, "The Four Horsemen." Although Metallica won't hit the stage for hours, the excitement is palpable among this hometown crowd of old thrashers, young longhairs, weekend warriors and metal chicks, all of whom have come to see Metallica kick out a fiery set of old and new favorites pulled from a quarter-century of classic metal—from their 1983 debut, *Kill 'Em All*, to 2008's epic *Death Magnetic*.

Since the release of 1991's chart-crushing Black Album, Metallica have enjoyed full-fledged global domination of the metal market. Yet, as expansive as their empire has become, there was a time back in the early Eighties when the SoCal four-piece was championed almost exclusively by a cult of adolescent males disaffected by mainstream music—a grassroots, tape-trading clique that related to Metallica's fast-as-hell riffs, boundless energy and boozy, kick-ass older brother persona.

Counted among those headbangers was Tool guitarist Adam Jones, who has followed the band ever since *Kill 'Em All*.

"They're still the 'older brothers,' " says Jones, who has accepted *Guitar World*'s offer to watch the sold-out show and catch up with his old friend Kirk Hammett. "The reason I like Metallica is because they're very complex, mature men who at the same time have the enthusiasm of little kids. There's nothing better than meeting your heroes and finding that they're real, down-to-earth people. You can go out and have a beer with them and talk about something besides, 'Oh, you're great. I love your band. I love that song.' You can forget all that and just have a really inspiring conversation."

Like Metallica, Tool insist on creating the music they want to hear, a progressively heady and utterly heavy sound that, as it turns out, many others want to hear. What's more, their willingness to challenge industry models and expectations has earned them the respect and devotion of fans, critics and artists alike. "I'm a *big* Tool fan. How could I not be?" Hammett announces when we sit down for our interview on the evening of the Forum show. "They have everything: riffs, arrangements and subject matter. They just kick ass, and they are definitely one of the best bands to come out in a long time."

As a testament to the loyalty of Tool fans, when the band released 2006's *10,000 Days* after a five-year gap between the previous album, *Lateralus*, the record immediately shot to Number One and eventually went Platinum. Tool are the rare band that can go up the mountain, disappear for years and return—with 10 (or so) commanding tracks— to an even stronger reception.

Intriguingly, Tool and Metallica took opposite attitudes toward building recognition when their popularity started to grow: Hammett and his bandmates became increasingly more visible; Tool obscured their faces in photo shoots and stopped appearing in videos. "When we first started out here in Hollywoodland," Jones explains, "we saw that everyone had to have a look. We decided that people would be more serious about listening to everything we did if they didn't know what we looked like. Early on Metallica had a bit of the Tool thing going in the fact that they weren't overly pumping their image. But because of their success, Metallica found themselves in the spotlight more than we were, to the point where they've now become iconic. But to me the music is what comes first. I remember hearing those first three Metallica albums. They were so good I didn't care what the band looked like!"

Given their similar experiences and mutual admiration for each other's bands, it's not surprising that Hammett and Jones connected when they first met in the Nineties. "We opened for Metallica in Korea and decided to hit Hawaii on our way back to do a couple shows," explains Jones. "Kirk was heading to Hawaii, too, but I didn't see him on our plane. After we landed, I was getting my luggage and I felt this tap on my shoulder. It was Kirk, and he said, 'Are you the guitarist in Tool? I love your band. Would you like to come to dinner?' And I was like, 'Yeah!' "

In the years since that first meeting, the two have cultivated a friendship built on a shared belief in art for art's sake—not to mention a love of seriously thrashing guitar work, classic prog-rock, esoteric subjects, comic books and surfing.

Having arrived a few minutes early for our interview, Adam and I are escorted down a ramp into the belly of the massive Forum and led to the room designated for our interview. No sooner do we sit down on a pair of leather couches than Hammett bursts through the door, clutching a freshly custom-painted ESP. The rapport between the two guitarists is apparent as they greet each other with smiles and hearty handshakes.

After a minute of ogling Kirk's occult-themed ax (more on that later), I sit down speak to the two guitarists about a range of topics, not the least of which is how to become a successful artist while staying true to your vision—a subject that both guitarists are uniquely qualified to discuss.

GUITAR WORLD Let's start with a little history. How did you guys become friends?

KIRK HAMMETT I've always admired Adam from a distance.

ADAM JONES A far distance.

HAMMETT As far a distance as possible. [*laughs*] We played some shows together in 2006, in Korea, and that's when we started getting to know each other. After those Korean shows, Tool went right to Hawaii. I was also going to Hawaii, because I spend a lot of time there.

They were playing a show, and Adam asked me to come onstage and play "Sober" with him. To which I said, "Hell yes!"

JONES Yeah, it was really great. We extended the breakdown in "Sober" where [*Tool vocalist*] Maynard [*James Keenan*] comes in by himself, and we built the song back up into the chorus again. We softly started playing the main riff and let Kirk swim over it. For a guy who didn't prepare at all, he blew my mind! It just kept getting better—more complex and cooler.

HAMMETT It was one of my best onstage jamming experiences, ever. It was totally improvised and really mind-blowing.

GW Adam, in the days before Tool did you ever listen to Metallica?

JONES Absolutely. You always hear about the prog and math stuff that influenced me, but there's also Aerosmith, AC/DC and Metallica. All that stuff has affected me. It's really funny to think back to when I bought *...And Justice for All*, that one day I would be hanging out or surfing with Kirk.

GW You guys surf together?

JONES Yeah. The first time was in Hawaii, the day after we met. He lent me a long board and took me out to this spot where all the old-timers surf. I'm from California, so I've never had to paddle 30 minutes *anywhere*. [*laughs*] And you have to go out real far in Waikiki to catch the good waves. My arms were getting so tired, and I was so worried I was gonna look like a pussy! [*laughs*]

GW What initially attracted you to Metallica's music?

JONES I definitely have this prog side of me, so I listen for counter rhythms and polyrhythms, and *...And Justice for All* had stuff in seven and nine. There's even one riff that's in 11, which I really like. But I'm sure you guys don't count it like that, or maybe you do?

HAMMETT I can only count to four, bro. [*laughs*]

JONES Exactly. [*laughs*] We actually do that too. We write weird riffs and sometimes we count them and other times we just feel them. I always felt that the stuff on ...*And Justice for All* was written from Metallica's heart and not their head.

GW Kirk, what do you like about Adam's playing?

HAMMETT I really appreciate that Adam is the prog master. I love the fact that he strives to create progressive music that really stands on its own. I come from a real old-school prog back-ground myself. I love bands like King Crimson, Yes and Genesis. I love Robert Fripp, and I know Adam loves Robert Fripp, as well. I think it's cool that he's carrying that torch.

GW Adam, what attracts you to these artists? Is it strictly their music, or are you also drawn to their ideologies or creative processes?

JONES If I have the chance to find out what David Bowie was thinking when he came up with this or that, I'm absolutely interested. But it's also nice to be immersed in just the song without worrying what it's about. That curiosity can backfire. The funniest time for me was when I found out what the Melvins song "Boris" was really about. It's from *Bullhead,* which is a very innovative and phenomenal record. I remember listening to the lyrics and being like, This is the purest, most meaningful and heaviest shit I've heard in a long time. Later on, after I befriended [*Melvins guitarist/singer*] Buzz [*Osborne*], I said, "That song 'Boris' really means a lot to me." And he says, "Oh, that song's about my cat." [*laughs*] So it's good to not get too analytical about this stuff.

> "I love the fact that Adam strives to create progressive music that **really stands on its own.**"
> —*HAMMETT*

GW Kirk, how much does musical analysis play a role in Metallica?

HAMMETT Adam really nailed it when he said some people count it and some people feel it. We *totally* feel it. You won't hear anyone in our band saying, "Oh that's in five and this is in seven." We'll say something like, "It's on the upbeat," "It's on the downbeat," "Switch here after you count to five"... It's really simple for us: it comes from the gut and heart rather than the head. Sometimes it does come from the head, and I have to sit down and do the math. But after I've done the math, I just start feeling it again.

> "It's important to remember where your head was when you first started."
> —*JONES*

JONES Thinking too much will always become distracting. When you think too much, especially when you start to get successful, you can go down paths like, Oh, what will the fans like? What will radio like? But when you keep it in your chest or stomach, it stays about What do *I* like? When you nail that, only then will your excitement be reflected by other people who listen to your music.

GW In the early days Metallica gained its rep and momentum through its cult status, with the tape traders and underground metalheads. Similarly, a cult of fans has always surrounded Tool. I'm wondering what, in your opinions, are the upsides and downsides to becoming a cult phenomenon?

JONES The upside is that you can play onstage and you can fart, and no one knows it. [*laughs*]

HAMMETT [*laughs*] I just totally lost my thought, because that statement was just so profound.

JONES [*laughs*] I know, sorry. I think the downside is that there's a real potential to forget your roots and why you started playing in the first place. It's important to remember where your head was when you first started, because when you get successful and spoiled it's easy to forget the excitement of when you were first writing songs. And that's why his band and my band go into hiding—to write songs and try to find that spot again. We do this so we don't just keep writing what we wrote last time that was successful and start sounding like a cover band of ourselves. We have to constantly go back and find ourselves.

HAMMETT I guess you can say *Death Magnetic* is Metallica reaching back to our cultish days, as well. I don't know if you can even call us a "cult band" now, because we're a very popular band. Can you be a cult band and still be popular? I don't know.

JONES It probably depends on who you ask. I think the word "cult" comes from an outsider's perspective. When someone on the outside looks at Metallica, they would say they have a cult following. Because Metallica have had years of success and have a dedicated fan base, it could almost seem like people are following them out of blind faith, but I don't think this is exactly correct. Tool has had that too. I've heard stuff like, "How can a band that a lot of people never heard of have Gold and Platinum records?" That's when they'll say, "It's because Tool has a weird cult following." To me it's just a term people use to describe something they don't quite know how to explain... which is not necessarily a bad thing.

GW It also seems a cult band can become an easy target for disgruntled fans when it grows beyond being their "pet band."

HAMMETT I know that a lot of people who are cultish types are really obsessive. They *really* want a certain thing, or feeling, and they find this thing in a band. When the band grows bigger—and maybe more personally inaccessible as a result—these cultish people try even harder to get this thing or feeling from the band. There's a certain type of person who is obsessed with Metallica who spends all of their time trying to get this one thing outta our music, and when they don't get it they become *passionately* pissed off. [*laughs*]

JONES For me, there's nothing wrong with obsession as long as you're getting something out of it that's positive. And when your expectations are let down because you didn't like this record as much as the last record...well, you just have to be a little more forgiving, or move on.

HAMMETT "Forgiving" is totally the right word, because after all it is just music. You *can* live through it.

HAMMETT Speaking of music, how's the new album coming along, Adam?

JONES It's coming along...great! [*laughs*] No, we've been on hiatus. I'm writing and [*bassist*] Justin [*Chancellor*]'s been writing, but Maynard has been working on his wine. [*Keenan owns the Caduceus Cellars winery in Arizona.*] We've all just been taking some time away from each other, which has been nice. I've also been working on producing some comics.

HAMMETT Ah, fantastic. Right on. I know last time we talked you were doing a Tool video.

JONES We're working on "The Pot," but I've been really lazy lately. [*laughs*] The setup for it is a lot more epic, so it's actually good that we've been able to have more time. It's going to be all stop-motion and in 3D. We're doing it so that we can hopefully have it shown in the theater.

HAMMETT Wow. With glasses and the whole thing?

JONES Yeah, because a lot more theaters are going digital and those projectors can do 3D. We have a consultant who worked with us on the 3D packaging for *10,000 Days*, and he was telling me that in 10 to 20 years you won't need goggles for 3D, you'll go to the movie theater and everything will look like 3D. It's almost holographic. It's really exciting. Sorry, gimme a chance to nerd out and I will. [*laughs*]

GW No sweat. Actually, let's nerd out on some music questions. Musical tension is a large component in both Tool and Metallica's sound. Kirk, Metallica are known for locked-down rhythms, which are balanced by your frenzied solos. As a guitarist do you see your role as a release for all the pent-up aggression?

HAMMETT Well, like I said earlier, I've always just felt the music. That's always been my approach. I've never put it under the microscope. My approach is to sit down and play, and whatever comes out is what I have to work with. But I do think I'm a very bombastic type of player. I have to try *really* hard to be subtle. Sometimes when the song calls for a section where I need to create a subtle atmosphere, I have trouble because there are all these explosions going off in my head. *Death Magnetic* is a good example of that: None of the solos are subtle! They're all just going for the throat. It's kinda just the way I play.

GW Your initial inspiration is spontaneous, but what specific techniques do you use to achieve maximum tension? Like maybe nailing a certain middle frequency on the wah?

HAMMETT Yeah, I use the wah in an unpredictable way. A lot of the reason why I love the wah is its unpredictability and randomness. You know that this tone will never be on that downbeat or that certain frequency will never be exactly at that microtone ever again.

JONES You mean there's more to the wah than using it for porno music?

HAMMETT [*imitating a porno wah sound*] Wack-a, wack-a, wack-a. [*laughs*] And as far as our songs are concerned, we just do what feels natural. When we're writing music—say when we're riding on a very heavy rhythmic riff—it's obvious to us where to go from there. Whether it's switching to half time with clean guitars or playing some arpeggiated chord thing with a key shift, those are some ways we create tension within a song.

JONES Your wah playing has influenced the way I approach the effect, especially the way that you use it as a wash. I love how you'll do a solo where you start real low on the wah and slowly bring it up. At least that's what I think you're doing.

HAMMETT Yeah, that's exactly it.

JONES I think it's cool, because most kids go out and buy one and immediately start playing the porno music. They don't think about how you can get the low tones without the high, and then you can go high and cut the low, which can really add a lot of emotion to what you're playing.

GW Adam, how do you go about adding tension to Tool's songs?

JONES My bandmates and I have never looked at songwriting like, There's verse, chorus, verse, chorus, breakdown, chorus, chorus, and it's three minutes long because that's what radio will play. Some songs have turned out like that, but we've never worried about it. My approach to playing, whether it's a riff or adding effects, has been, How can I build this? How can I take this from zero to 10 and make it more and more exciting? I've been a fan of the Melvins since before our band took off, and they've influenced me a lot. The biggest thing I've learned from them is the discipline of nothing—of negative space. Not playing between parts can be just as powerful as playing. Learning that taught me a lot about discipline, and I'm lucky, because everyone in Tool understands that sometimes less is more. It's like film: you have to build a moment and carry yourself toward it. You choose your own path. Do you take the short or long path? Is it a gravel or dirt road?

HAMMETT I've just got to say to Adam, I think the way you dial in certain colors with effects is really admirable. How you implement the filters and pedals into your music adds so much color to the sound.

JONES It's like you were saying, it's all about asking, "What does this part of the song need?" And that's what keeps it exciting, which in turn adds to the emotion and makes it more intense. That variety means so much more to me than, Oh, I hope Kirk plays the same exact solo on this song, too. Instead you hope he's going to take the emotion of the current song and enhance it through his lead playing.

GW I understand you two share similar tastes in visual art.

HAMMETT Absolutely. We have a similar sort of aesthetic with art, comic books, graphics and that whole deal.

JONES Watch out, our nerd sides are definitely coming out. [*laughs*] As soon as I started making any real money, I began investing in art, buying paintings, sculptures and original comic pages. Kirk and I bonded on that immediately, because he has a huge appreciation of art. I will vindictively hate Kirk for the rest of my life because he owns a bunch of [*original works by fantasy illustrator/painter*] Frank Frazetta. [*laughs*]

HAMMETT I also have a big fascination with the occult and esoteric subjects. I know Adam is into sacred geometry [*the relationship between mathematical ratios and music, architecture, cosmology and so on*], which is something I'm way into, too, as well as quantum physics and all that sort of stuff. So we're connecting on quite a few levels.

GW Speaking of mysterious subject matter, Kirk, you brought a pretty tripped-out ESP guitar with you today, which goes well with this issue's cult heroes theme.

HAMMETT More like *occult* heroes. [*laughs*] Basically, for this guitar, I gave the artist [*American painter*] Mark Ryden a list of topics, and I said, "Translate these ideas into your vision and paint it onto the guitar." There's a bee, which is symbolic of knowledge; the raven, symbolizing secret knowledge; and then the all-seeing eye, symbolic of universal knowledge. Caduceus [*a symbol formed by a short staff entwined by two serpents*] symbolizes the tree of life, but if you notice it also resembles a DNA strand [*a double helix*]. Then there's the hand from heaven, the Rosicrucian rose and my astrological sign, Scorpio, as well as assorted skulls and a yin-yang. It's *full* of numerology, astrology, occult and religious symbolism.

JONES It's an amazing-looking guitar. I love all the light sources beaming off of the female shape, and the design at the center, over the pickups, which I see as a life-and-death thing. Mark Ryden is really the icon of this current underground, up-and-coming art movement, and he's paved the way for a lot of people who have similar approaches. I've seen his paintings in person in Seattle, and he is a master at what he does. I'm glad he's now getting the recognition. And Kirk's going to play it and scratch it all up? He should just put it under glass and hang it on his wall. Or better yet, give it to me. [*laughs*]

HAMMETT It's gonna see some wear and tear, but that's its purpose. Plus, Mark said he'd do touch-ups when they're needed.

GW It seems you're both very thoughtful when it comes to studying hermetic philosophies. Do you find them useful in adding order to your lives outside of the musical realm, too?

JONES The order is already there. It's just that we're making ourselves aware of it. Sacred geometry is basically studying anything and breaking it down to its purist form, be it a symbol, shape, color, vibration or sound. That's what our life is. It goes outside who we are as people, the earth or the universe, into the spiritual realm or even an unconscious collective realm.

GW Going back to your guitar, Kirk, what specifically fascinates you about symbolism?

HAMMETT Well, as far as symbolism goes, there are different schools of thought, like how colors can influence your mood or perspective. Different symbols, like the all-seeing eye or the rose, will trigger different things in your psyche or unconscious. All this stuff is influential on some level and has an impact on the person surveying it, whether on a quantum level or a more overt level. I'm really interested in that sort of thing. Another good example of this is Jimmy Page's use of the ZoSo sigil, which

> "For me, music is vibration, and the universe seems to be created based on numbers and vibrations."
> —*HAMMETT*

he had written on his outfit. [*A sigil is a word or symbol of supposed occult power. Page's ZoSo symbol first appeared on the packaging of* Led Zeppelin IV *and later on his stage outfits.*] He thought that it helped his music and artistic direction. I'm totally into how certain images can influence the subconscious mind. On a very basic level, if this guitar was stark white I would feel completely different about it. The fact that it has this amazing graphic on it inspires me and moves me.

GW Does this kind of energy transfer relate to your belief in string theory and the effect of vibrations, which you've talked to us about before? [*String theory is a model in physics proposing that all elementary particles are manifestations of the vibrations of one-dimensional strings.*]

HAMMETT For me, music is vibration, and the universe seems to be created based on numbers and vibrations. If you want to get down to quantum physics, string theory and other dimensions, it seems to me that vibration is what holds the entire universe together. The fact that we're musicians and we use vibrations to conjure up moods, atmospheres, emotions, thoughts and concepts—well, a lot of times I think musicians are magicians in that sense! But I'm just getting way out there on the ledge now. [*laughs*]

JONES No, you're absolutely right. There's an emotional bond that Kirk's talking about that comes from what influences him and what influences me. That kind of bond is partially why I think Metallica are so successful. The four members are very different from each other, but they bring all these different perspectives and influences together and meet in the middle—and then it becomes something else altogether. I think that's why their music is incredibly eclectic. I think of the Black Album and how no two songs sound the same.

I love my bandmates in Tool for that same reason: we all think about where things come from. Like I was talking about before with sacred geometry: if you can break something down into its basic form—like the vibrations Kirk mentions—and you can apply that to what you do, then people will get it, without even knowing they're getting it! There's a harmonic vibration that reaches out and affects people consciously or unconsciously. I'm completely inspired by this type of thinking, including Kirk's views of the universe, and what I talk about as the "unconscious collective" and how all the different perceptions are interwoven. It's almost like a sweater: there are many different threads along different paths, but they are all woven together. It's a nice way of looking at the perception of things.